WOMEN, POWER AND THE ACADEMY
From Rhetoric to Reality

Edited by *Mary-Louise Kearney*

Berghahn Books
New York • Oxford

UNESCO Publishing
PARIS

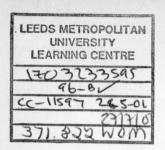
Published jointly by
the **United Nations Educational, Scientific and Cultural Organization**
and by
Berghahn Books

© 2000 UNESCO

Library of Congress Cataloging-in-Publication Data

Women, power and the academy : from rhetoric to reality / edited by Mary-Louise Kearney.
  p. cm.
"Book was inspired by the outcomes of the thematic debate on Women and Higher Education: Issues
and Perspectives, which took place at the World Conference on Higher Education, Paris, 1998"-Pref.
Includes bibliographical references.
ISBN 1-57181-247-4 (alk. paper)--ISBN 1-57181-248-2 (pb. : alk. paper)
  1. Women--Education (Higher)--Cross-cultural studies--Congresses. 2. Feminism and education--
Cross-cultural studies--Congresses. I. Kearney, Mary-Louise.

LC1551 . W66 2000
371.822- -dc21

                                                                                      00-045495

British Library Cataloguing in Publication Data

A catalogue record for this book is available from the British Library.

Printed in Great Britain by Polestar Scientifica

              ISBN UNESCO: 92–3–103758-7
              ISBN Berghahn: 1-57181-247-4 hardback
              ISBN Berghahn: 1–57181–248–2 paperback

*The designations employed and the presentation of material throughout this publication do not
imply the expression of any opinion whatsoever on the part of the UNESCO Secretariat concerning the legal status of any country, territory, city or area or of its authorities, or the delineation of
its frontiers or boundaries.*
*The authors are responsible for the choice and the presentation of the facts contained in this book
and for the opinions expressed therein, which are not necessarily those of UNESCO and do not
commit the Organization.*

CONTENTS

TABLES, FIGURES AND CHARTS

Tables

Figures

Charts

PREFACE

This book was inspired by the outcomes of the thematic debate on Women and Higher Education: Issues and Perspectives, which took place at the World Conference on Higher Education, Paris, 1998. This debate was sponsored by the Swedish International Development Cooperation Agency.

The conference aimed to set the major orientations for the renovation of higher education in the twenty-first century. For this, a new vision and approach to all areas of this sector are needed. The debate presented a critical appraisal of women's status quo with regard to their access to higher education, their presence in the academy and in institutional management, and their role in the development of their local and national societies.

The views presented by the international panelists and participants resulted in unanimous agreement on the need for additional change and action to promote the advancement of women in higher education and in the development process, to ensure their enhanced presence in decision-making structures and to remove any cultural barriers impeding their progress.

Although these objectives may be simply stated, in reality they are complex to attain. This book is a collection of essays on aspects of this complexity. As such, it constitutes an original contribution to the ongoing quest for full gender equality in society.

We would like to thank the authors for sharing their valuable reflections and the Inter-American Organization for Higher Education for its generous support.

Linda Souter
President, International Federation of University Women

NOTES ON CONTRIBUTORS

Nina Arnhold, a teacher and researcher, has just completed a doctorate in higher education at Oxford University

Sheryl Bond is a researcher at Queen's University, Canada, and co-ordinated the women's programme for the Inter-American Organization for Higher Education

Abdalla Bubtana, Libya, directs UNESCO's Doha Office and represents the Organization in the Arab States of the Gulf

Maria Inácia D'Ávila Neto and **Cíntia Simões Pires** are professors of Social Psychology at the Federal University of Rio de Janeiro, Brazil

Anne Holden Rønning is professor of English Literature at the University of Bergen, Norway

Peter Katjavivi is Vice-Chancellor of the University of Namibia

Mary-Louise Kearney is head of the Unit for the World Conference on Higher Education, UNESCO

Binod Khadria is professor of Social Sciences at the Jawaharlal Nehru University, New Delhi, India

Judith Mbula Bahemuka is professor of Sociology at the University of Nairobi, Kenya, and co-ordinator of the UNESCO Chair in Women and Community Health

Ralitsa Muharska directs the Women's Studies Programme at the St Kliment Ochrid University, Sofia, Bulgaria

Robyn Munford and **Sylvia Rumball** hold executive academic and administrative posts at Massey University, New Zealand

Berit Olsson is Director of Cooperation at the Swedish International Development Cooperation Agency and **Christina Ullenius** is President of the University of Karlstad, Sweden

Sylvia Perry is immediate past President of the International Federation of Business and Professional Women

Susan Van der Vynckt, USA, is UNESCO's Senior Education Adviser for Africa

Project Manager: *Liliana Simionescu*
Research: *Sylvie Brochu*

OVERVIEW: FROM RHETORIC TO REALITY

Mary-Louise Kearney

Introduction

We cannot end the century with 90 per cent of decisions made by men. Let us follow this empowerment – this 'in-powerment'. We are in a moment of vision – we can pass to action if we have the political will.

These words come from the debate on Women and Higher Education at the World Conference on Higher Education (WCHE), Paris, 1998. They vividly express the paradox that characterizes the issue of gender in this sector. Strong support for the principle is voiced by every government and every group of stakeholders. Indeed, the Declaration and Framework for Priority Action, adopted at the World Conference, paid due attention to the issue of gender equality in higher education. However, the reality of women's advancement towards empowerment, both in this sector and in society, continues to be very slow.

Why is this so? One of the questions discussed at the World Conference was that of the critical-mass factor. However, is this a reliable indicator? Do the increased numbers of educated women mean that their empowerment – *and their ' in-powerment'* – are inevitable? These are dangerous assumptions, as empowerment and in-powerment appear to remain two quite separate concepts.

As women continue to advance in every field of endeavour, the impression that equality has been reached has naturally gained ground. Some might even argue – out of personal conviction or optimism, or by quoting positive evidence – that the gender issue no longer poses a real problem. More women are entering education at all levels, and consequently acquiring the capacities needed to succeed in different walks of life. In the area of higher education, this enhanced entry should lead to their stronger presence in the professions and at the highest echelons of social decision-making, where the role played by graduates has always been predominant. The critical mass has already become a reality in many contexts and is on the way to becoming a reality in others. In the not-too-distant future, the numbers of women should equal those of men possessing the skills necessary to shape social-development processes.

Unfortunately, this rhetoric is not matched by reality. The reaction of participants at the World Conference debate to this type of discourse was dubious, and they resolved to analyse why this argument must be refuted. Why are attitudes to gender equality not changing fast enough? Why are women prevented from participating fully in social decision-making? How does this inequality impact on the challenges facing the higher-education sector?

These are complex questions that cannot be answered by quoting the inevitable advent of the critical mass, at which time, supposedly, all problems will magically disappear. Rather, to move towards deeper understanding of this continuing inequality, some reflection on key concepts is needed – e.g., the nature of cultural traditions, the meaning of empowerment and of power-sharing, of feminine leadership, and the culture of higher education itself. Such reflection will certainly challenge established views on women and power across regions and their peoples. However, without such analysis, no genuine progress from rhetoric to reality will take place.

Culture, Women and Power

> *Gender is one of the issues that concerns every culture; gender issues have turned out to be among the most sensitive ones in a changing world, since any transformation in this realm inevitably disrupts the patterns of identity of both genders and touches upon issues of dominance – and hence of power.*
>
> Our Cultural Diversity, 1996, p. 28

The World Commission on Culture and Development, convened by UNESCO and chaired by Javier Perez de Cuellar, tackled issues of great complexity because they challenged the belief that social progress is a simple linear path to be trod by all nations, regardless of their widely differing cultural heritages and traditions. Indeed, the concept of development was broadened from mere economic considerations to embrace a myriad of aspects that concern all groups and dimensions of society: *inter alia*, health, education, the environment, the media, and the needs of young people and of women. With the advent of globalization, awareness of the reality of cultural pluralism now permeates national cultural policies. The world is a village where all peoples must live and advance together for their common benefit, but in distinctive ways.

Culture, then, in the anthropological sense, signifies recognition and respect for the specific identity and way of life of a people or of a society. The

Commission further linked this definition of culture to the notion of human development, as proposed by the United Nations Development Programme (UNDP). This privileges the search for human dignity and well-being through enlarging people's choices to pursue endeavours that both reflect their personal values and shape their roles in society.

Culture and gender

The Commission confirmed that development processes are changing perceptions of men's and women's life cycles and of their respective patterns of participation in society. As nations recognize the principle of gender equality, so they must commit themselves to women's advancement in concrete ways – through legislation to safeguard rights, and through measures to redistribute income, assets and social power. But attitudes to these areas alter across different cultures.

Gender has thus become a highly politicized domain, and one characterized by paradox. As a result of globalization, women are now widely recognized as full actors in development. At the same time, a new emphasis has been laid on cultural specificity, since women are often depicted as symbols of their spiritual and social heritages. Consequently, development agendas today must be extremely sensitive to cultural factors. It is essential to avoid a bias that is predominantly Western and thus ethnocentric; yet, if the pernicious effects of cultural relativism gain ground, then women risk being deprived of their basic rights through an erroneous citation of difference.

In the Commission's view, in order to ensure that the gender dimension is correctly incorporated into the cultural fabric of each and every society, policy should be revised in four priority areas to ensure: (1) the recognition of women's rights as human rights; (2) women's reproductive freedom; (3) gender-aware planning of all projects and programmes; and (4) enhanced civic and cultural participation of women in all walks of life.

Cultural barriers to empowerment

The actual barriers preventing women's progress have long been identified, notably: (1) limited access to education, including advanced studies; (2) discriminatory appointments and promotion practices in the workplace; (3) the stresses of dual domestic and professional roles; (4) family attitudes; (5) career interruptions; (6) cultural stereotyping; (7) alienation from the male-dominated management culture (and continued resistance to admitting women to managerial positions); (8) continued propagation of the glass-ceiling syndrome and of covert practices for advancement; and (9) absence of adequate policies and legislation to protect women's rights.

The women's debate at the World Conference on Higher Education tended to take a new perspective on these obstacles, seeing them as resulting essentially from cultural attitudes rather than from social or economic conditions. Of course, the latter areas continue to pose many problems. For example, many women are obliged to cope with the pressures of home and workplace for primarily financial reasons, and often at the expense of quality of lifestyle and family relationships.

However, to describe these barriers as 'cultural' derives from the belief that attitude can help resolve many problematical situations. Key questions to be considered include: How are women perceived in different cultures? How do women see themselves and their range of choices as citizens? What pressures come to bear if cultural traditions are challenged or not respected?

These are complex areas that hold great sway over women's capacity to advance. For example, in certain contexts – including, but not limited to, the developing world – higher education for women wins approval while they await a socially acceptable marriage – but they are never seriously expected to apply their qualifications in a professional activity. In contrast, in Western settings where women are well integrated into the landscape of work, it is still felt – usually by the women workers themselves – that the feminine voice is not really heard; that women must perform better; and that, more often than not, the old-boy network will finally prevail whenever a choice must be made between male and female colleague for an appointment or promotion.

Last, but not least, one important cultural barrier is women's personal perceptions of their expectations from life – both personally and professionally. If they are conditioned by cultural backgrounds and attitudes to accept stereotyped roles, limited perspectives and a status inferior to that of their male counterparts, then they become the authors of their own fates. Self-esteem and self-confidence, often nurtured through positive family and educational environments, are indispensable attributes for women when obliged to explain and defend their choices, as they will surely be required to do throughout their lives.

Power, leadership and gender

Power, it must be recalled, must be in balance with related concepts, notably, authority, domination, responsibility and collaboration. Absolute power will certainly corrupt because it knows no limits of application or consequence. To quote an expert opinion on leadership: 'The danger of pathology is always present. Many leaders, when they acquire a position of power and authority, lose a sense of boundaries, not realizing the impact they have on other people in the organization' (Kets De Vries, 1993, p. xvii).

For centuries, the world has grown too accustomed to domination, conflict and internecine struggles for total control that brook no opposition or contrary viewpoint, elimination of opponents and the proliferation of win/lose scenarios. History is scattered with the destructive results of discord, violence and outright confrontation. Few are the leaders whose concern for their 'flocks' (whether constituencies, shareholders, family members or office colleagues) can be described as benign and lacking self-interest. And yet people seek leadership – a strong presence that provides a picture of the way forward and how to move there. Leaders must focus on the task at hand, while exhorting people to recognize a higher purpose that elevates their tasks, however important or menial these may be.

Power is an ambiguous sphere, and not for the faint-hearted. To command respect and affection, the sense of self is vital. Positive feelings of confidence and worth must be balanced with critical analysis, humility and a commitment to better performance as a service to humankind.

Higher-education governance is an area undergoing rapid change. The previous model of an institutional leader who was an academic *primus inter pares* has given way to the management ethic, which demands a panoply of much broader skills. A desirable profile would list some, perhaps all, of the following attributes: (1) a strong academic profile; (2) leadership and visioning ability; (3) management skills; (4) wide institutional experience; (5) international experience of higher-education provision; (6) negotiating capacities for internal and external purposes; (7) excellent communication abilities; and (8) charisma (if possible).

Quite clearly, the emphasis on managerial skills equals that placed on pure 'brain power'. As a result of this change in profile for institutional leadership, potential candidates seek rapid acquisition of the necessary attributes through tailor-made management training.

Leadership is thus a multifaceted concept comprising, *inter alia*, vision, the ability to inspire and to organize (often contradictory), to cope with real power, and to shoulder responsibility – and, through these talents, to serve social progress rather than a personal agenda. Furthermore, leadership in the global society has created new criteria, such as a capacity to steer ahead in a climate of chaos and a flexibility sensitive to an important range of multiple factors.

Against this background, women leaders have, until now, tended to fall into two distinct categories. The first group comprises those who are willing to play the power game by men's rules. Such women are usually mentored by a powerful man and offer few, if any, opportunities for advancement to other women. Ruthlessness is a significant trait of those who do not seek new ways of sharing responsibility and authority. The other group, however, includes those who have sought to develop a concept of feminine leadership that can be practised and enjoyed by both genders because it privileges equal development rather than rivalry. Feminine leadership emphasizes: (1) a commitment to power-sharing; (2) an insistence on self-respect and merit; (3) a focus on concrete results; and (4) accommodation of the numerous pressures faced by managers.

Frequently, women from all cultures are awed by the complexity of assets required by the modern leader. Yet, ironically, they themselves frequently possess these skills, honed by years of expertise in managing personal relationships and the constant negotiation this implies. In short, women are generally much better equipped for leadership and responsibility than they would believe, through their natural roles as spouses, mothers and caregivers. Society at large is in dire need of such attributes, and for these to be evident in the decision-making arenas. Women are often too slow to realize their own potential, and that 'influences which lead to discovery are not merely scholarly but include the personality, life experiences and cultural context' (Bond, 1997, p. 5).

Women leaders, therefore, are created by several forces, of which advanced learning is just one element. Indeed, such a suggestion seems naive, although 'education' in the fullest sense of the term has a crucial place in moulding such persons. Empowerment and in-powerment now imply innovative approaches to authority, while, at the same time, upholding a sense of social responsibility. Women everywhere, through their multiple roles, are highly accustomed to dealing with this challenge. Those – either men or other women – who deny this opportunity are guilty of discrimination and old-fashioned thinking. If these attitudes prevail, society will not progress.

Empowering Women

> *Begin with the human being: with the capacities and needs that join all humans, across barriers of gender and class and race and nation.... The concept of the human being has already been central to much of the best feminist and internationalist thinking.*
> *Women, Culture and Development, pp. 61,63*

Defining women's empowerment

The words of the distinguished American scholar, Martha Nussbaum, reaffirm that the development process is primarily a *human* matter. It thus concerns both men and women, and the fundamental equality of their rights as they strive for democracy, education, health, employment and all other aspects of social progress. Empowerment is essentially a matter of rights – the recognition and possession of these, and the ability to enjoy them in a spirit of freedom and responsibility.

Crucial to the successful definition and recognition of women's rights as basic human rights are the various international protocols that set down the key principles of equality, non-discrimination and inclusion. Important instruments include: the Universal Declaration of Human Rights, 1948; the Convention against Discrimination in Education, 1960; and the Convention on the Elimination of All Forms of Discrimination against Women,

1979. These are complemented by the declarations and outcomes of the major conferences (for example, The World Conference on Education for All, Jomtien, Thailand, 1990; The United Nations Conference on Environment and Development, Rio de Janeiro, 1992; Population and Development, Cairo, 1994; the World Social Summit, Copenhagen, 1995; Habitat II, Istanbul, 1996; and Cultural Policies for Development, Stockholm, 1998; and decades (for examples, Cultural Development 1988-97, and Human Rights 1995-2004).

Of course, a special role has been played by the four World Conferences on Women in Mexico (1975), Copenhagen (1980), Nairobi (1985) and Beijing (1995). These have been landmarks in the struggle to bring the status of women, the issues that shape their lives, and the gender dimension to the forefront of public attention for corrective action.

In particular, the Beijing Platform of Action, adopted at the 1995 Fourth World Conference on Women, lists ongoing areas of concern for women: (1) their poverty and unequal access to social services; (2) their vulnerability to violence; (3) their absence from social and economic decision-making and power structures; (4) society's failure to recognize their rights; (5) the image of women in the media; and (6) insufficient mechanisms to promote their advancement.

Although a quarter of a century has elapsed since the first conference in Mexico, the cause is far from won. Constant vigilance, advocacy and activism remain necessary. Attitudes will have to undergo major change if we are to move from rhetoric to reality with regard to true equality. Debates on women may feature in the programme of every major conference, but, according to Linda Souter, President of the International Federation of University Women, gender issues and perspectives should be discussed as an integral part of every session of the conference, and not in a separate forum where the audience is predominantly female. Until this is the case, real equality has not been attained, and the gender dimension remains a marginal and often misunderstood concept.

Participation as an indicator of empowerment

A recurrent observation in the recent literature on women's advancement and equality is the importance of their presence and participation. Unless they are fully involved in social and economic decision-making, then the voice of 50 per cent of humanity is not heard. Sometimes this presence will bring strong criticism – for example, the recent enfranchisement of women in Kuwait. There may even be an undesirable backlash whereby attitudes harden against the progress of women. Yet, it must be hoped that these setbacks will be temporary, and that the overall tide of justice will prevail.

Where do women rank in various key areas of social activity?

Table A. *Women Parliamentarians*

High human-development countries	
Canada	21.2%
Norway	36.4%
Costa Rica	15.8%
Hungary	11.4%

Medium human-development countries	
Botswana	8.5%
Cuba	22.8%
Egypt	2.0%
Turkey	2.4%

Low human-development countries	
India	7.3%
Haiti	3.6%
Mali	12.2%
Sudan	5.3%

When aggregated, the figures for women in parliament rise to:	
All developing countries	8.6%
Industrialized countries	15.3%
The world	11.8%

(Source: Human Development Report, 1998)

Table B. *Women in Government*

	Total per cent	Percentages at ministerial level	Percentages at sub-ministerial level
All developing countries	5%	5%	5%
Industrialized countries	13%	11%	13%
The world	7%	7%	7%

(Source: Human Development Report, 1997, 1998)

Table C. *Women in the Labour Force*

	Female percentages of labour force	
	1980	*1996*
World	39%	40%
Low-income countries	40%	40%
Middle-income countries	37%	38%
High-income countries	38%	43%

(Source: World Development Indicators, 1998)

Table D. *Women's Economic Participation*

	Country human-development index-rank percentages		
	High	Medium	Low
Administration/ Management	18%	13%	4%
Professional/Technical Fields	46%	44%	22%
Clerical/Sales	47%	38%	NA
Services	56%	48%	NA

(Source: Table 11, Human Development Report, 1997)

The following table indicates the low number of high-level women executives appointed to selected American companies in 1993:

Table E. *Women Business Executives*

	Executives	
Company	*Total*	*Women*
Ameritech	18	2
Chrysler Corp.	36	0
Comerica, Inc.	20	1
Ford Motor Co.	72	2
General Motors Corp.	58	3

(Source: Statistical Record of Women Worldwide, 1995)

These indicators attest both to the presence of women and to the unevenness of their presence. For instance, they figure strongly in the service area of employment, where work is often temporary; they also form the critical mass at the bottom end of each category of worker. In contrast, their numbers as parliamentarians vary greatly, while their numbers in posts of responsibility in government and in executive business are uniformly low. In other words, women may be present but fewer rise to posts of decision-making and responsibility. Indeed, the continuation of this trend is cause for concern and, according to Attiya Inayatullah, a former Pakistani minister and President of UNESCO's Executive Board, the question arises as to whether women really do have career paths. Thus, depending on where the presence of women is located in various domains attests to their empowerment in terms of significant numbers – and also to their very limited in-powerment when these numbers are small. In the latter instance, the dangers of tokenism and of symbolic participation are recalled.

The shift towards empowerment is a challenge to be addressed by education because of its role, at the grass-roots level, in the overall capacity-building of citizens. This will be a particular hurdle for universities to surmount since, though female enrolments have soared in all regions of the world, the power structures of these institutions remain very male-dominated. However, major changes are underway in education, including the sub-sector of advanced learning. As education becomes universalized in terms of the numbers admitted, so provision must alter, resulting in an attitudinal shift as traditional methods of teaching and learning are renovated.

Thus, despite the radical changes under way, education must continue to be a prime force in the empowerment of people as citizens. Yet, with regard to women's in-powerment, it cannot be ignored that other forces often play attendant – and equally effective – roles.

Capacity-building via education

Recognizing the principle of equal rights is just the first step. The next is acknowledging that, in many situations, this principle does not operate in practice for women. This is frequently due to the fact that women's capacities are less than those of men – for example, they may have fewer legal rights, reduced access to health care and education, and inferior salaries. Simply put, their lack of capacities to claim their rights is the origin of their inequality. As human beings, women merit the same opportunities to develop these capacities as men. Unless this is so, feminine injustice becomes an instance of human injustice. Capacity-building then moves centre-stage as the prime means of people's empowerment as citizens and professionals who can shape their own destinies and those of their different societies.

Education is generally seen as the main force for capacity-building. At one end of the scale, basic education is essential to equip people with fundamental knowledge, information and life skills. As such, its role in poverty alleviation is a tenet of the development discourse. At the other end is higher education, which has traditionally moulded the intellects of social leaders. In the past, these sectors have been viewed *vertically* – thus emphasizing the difference in educational provision for the haves and the have-nots. Rarely did one level lead to another, and the connection between them was all but disregarded. However, as education has become accessible to greater numbers of the population, the vertical vision has shifted to a *horizontal* approach. This stresses the equality of all types of educational provision, the closer links that necessarily exist amongst these and the facilitation of access across this spectrum. As a result, capacity-building concerns the entire education system and whole populations. There is no place for gender inequality in terms of access and participation. Women, like men, must be able to enjoy the full benefits deriving from the development of their specific capacities.

When we turn to the field of higher education, the role of capacity-building becomes more complex. This is due to several factors arising from the profound changes now occurring in this sector. An analysis of the trends must be focused on the core issue – namely, the demand for access in order to meet the requirements of living and working in today's knowledge-oriented society.

The 1998 report by the Organisation for Economic Co-operation and Development (OECD), *Redefining Tertiary Education,* remarks that 'access means *entry*

> not merely to an institution but to a way of life, not for the few but for all …. Society needs capable and responsible citizens performing a multitude of adult roles in a civilized fashion, and it needs many more people with these qualities and interests' (OECD, 1998, pp. 37, 38).

This statement implies that the sea change now occurring in post-secondary education must be gender-inclusive. The purposes and methods of this sector must alter radically if it is to meet the challenges of the next century and play its part in the development process as expected. Put simply, this means that systems and institutions of higher learning must be perceived by governments as real and effective partners. Today, we face a situation of paradox that must be reconstructed for positive ends. On one hand, national authorities are grappling with complex socio-economic and cultural issues; on the other hand, higher-education systems are actors in the production and dissemination of advanced knowledge. The solutions found must benefit all citizens – men and women alike.

The World Conference on Higher Education sought to address the main issues related to change and development in this sector. The overall aims of the conference were the promotion of access on merit, the renovation of systems and institutions of higher education, and their closer linkages with the world of work. These concerns were analysed throughout the conference in various sessions: the ministerial plenary discussions, the commission programme and the thematic debates.

Today, as nations seek to adapt to a society based on knowledge, education and training have become priority policy issues. In a paper commissioned by the World Bank for the World Conference on Higher Education,

Chart A. *Old and new paradigms of knowledge-generation*

Old paradigm	New paradigm
generated in academic institutions	produced in the context of application
disciplinary	transdisciplinary
requires homogenous skills	needs heterogenous skills
hierarchically managed	diverse in organization
structured to respect traditional academic practice	promotes enhanced social accountability
peer-evaluated	broader quality-control mechanisms

(Source: Gibbons, 1998)

Michael Gibbons presented a paradigm of the old and new forms of knowledge generation:
The new paradigm also means that greater attention must be paid to the requirements of all the actors involved, whatever their gender. Learner profiles and needs are changing dramatically – a reality that systems and institutions can no longer ignore.

The final objective is to train self-reliant citizens and professionals of both sexes, as they represent a country's greatest asset in dealing with rapid social change. Thus, traditional academe must give way to greater diversification of educational purpose, with the empowerment of people being the overall concern.

Challenges for Universities

Today, the typical managerial figure in a university is the chief executive/vice-chancellor on a six-figure salary, brandishing a strategic plan and without high level academic achievement of his (still much less frequently her) own (Smith and Webster, 1997, p. 2).

Against the changing background of post-secondary educational provision, universities today face specific challenges: firstly, in their governance and management strategies, and secondly, in their missions to teach, train and research. In both instances, and notwithstanding the reactions from diverse cultural contexts, the gender dimension as a means of empowering women has its rightful place.

Women as institutional leaders

The small instance of institutions led by women is a sad reality for all regions. At present, more women sit in the world's parliaments and legisla-

Table F. *Percentages of universities worldwide run by women*

University associations	Members	Run by women (Number or %)
Africa	120	6
Arab States	103	2
Commonwealth	463	37
French-speaking	270	5–7%
Europe	497	6–8%
Asia/Pacific	140	5%
The Americas	350	5%
Latin America	177	47

(Source: 1998 figures from university non-governmental organizations)

tive assemblies than lead universities and other institutions of advanced study. A look at the figures for universities provides telling evidence:

Professorial and remunerative status

There is a continuing challenge for truly equal employment conditions for academic staff to be realized. In this context, women constitute a small and fragile minority.

The *professorial status* of female academics remains unacceptably low. Worldwide, women average only about 7 per cent of professorial posts. Though they are present in the humanities, they are notably absent in the sciences, indicating a clear instance of inequality. Thus, the ongoing research on factors influencing women's choices of studies should be given a high profile. Much has already been learnt about the shaping of attitudes early in life and about the pressures – often covert – faced by women who enter male-dominated fields. For example, a recent study in the United Kingdom showed that this country's average was 9.2 per cent for female professorships – by proportion, 20.1 per cent were found in education but only 2.1 per cent in engineering. The average figure means that 90.8 per cent of professorial appointments are held by men – thus recalling the remark of Federico Mayor that male domination in decision-making processes must be corrected.

In contrast, the numbers of women in the lower categories of personnel immediately increase. A survey conducted by the American Association of University Professors to illustrate the concentration of women by rank showed that, for 1997-98, they constituted 18.7 per cent of professors but 55.6 per cent of lecturers – thus, their numbers had tripled at this lower level.

The other areas where women in higher education are disadvantaged is in their *remuneration*. For example, in 1998, American male academics were paid more than their female counterparts: +12 per cent for professors; +3.45 per cent for associate professors; +6.4 per cent for assistant professors; +3.8 per cent for instructors. Moreover, salary-gender disparity had actually increased over the preceding 20 years. In terms of equal employment opportunity, this is clearly unjust.

Universities thus have the dubious privilege of likely remaining the most male-dominated establishments in the world in relation to career advancement. In an era in which gender equality is a key policy objective for the vast majority of governments, this reality is out of step with modern thinking, and cannot be considered as a source of pride for universities since such inequality does nothing to empower women in the academy itself. This lack of concordance between universities and other major social institutions is a serious matter for reflection and redress.

It is urgent to find remedies to the ills of gender imbalance in the university context. But, practically, what can be done? Gender equality must constitute a tenet of institutional mission. International and regional rectors' associations have a responsibility to promote this principle amongst their members. Gender equality can be an inherent part of institutional management through establishing an equal employment opportunities policy to ensure that the interests of women administrators, academics and students receive fair consideration. At the grass-roots level, the gender dimension of enrolment patterns, and course content and delivery can be an effective way of proving institutional commitment to relevance in higher education.

Relevance and the gender dimension

Until now, the university dilemma – namely, the impact of mass higher education in time-honoured traditions – has been experienced most commonly and with considerable pain in the industrialized countries. This dilemma is now evident in the developing world, where universities are being urged to direct their energy for teaching, training and research towards assuring a greater degree of pertinence in the provision of higher learning. Everywhere, unless this relevance is clearly perceived by the local community and linked national development priorities, higher education risks losing vital support from key stakeholders.

Indeed, relevance emerged as a key theme at the World Conference on Higher Education, whose Declaration defined this concept as:

> the fit between what society expects of institutions and what they do ... and a better articulation with the problems of society and the world of work, basing long-term orientations on societal aims and needs, including respect for cultures.... (Article. 6).

Today, more and more women are participating in higher education. In the industrialized countries, where student profiles are changing at a rapid pace, women now enrol more frequently – both in the traditional student cohort and as older and second-chance learners. In the developing world, the percentage of women students at the tertiary level has increased dramatically over the past decade as a result of their enhanced presence in secondary education. This stronger presence is a worldwide trend, as statistics confirm.

Table G. *Female enrolments in tertiary education*

| | *Female gross-enrolment ratio percentages* | |
	1985	*1995*
Australia	27.0	73.5
Austria	24.3	44.3
Chile	13.7	26.0
Tunisia	4.0	11.5
Zambia	0.6	1.4

(Source: World Education Report, 1998)

More research will be required to assess the impact of this feminization of the learner population, viz. their choice of studies, their success in male-dominated fields, and their particular pedagogical needs and expectations. These data will be needed to ensure the relevance of their courses and qualifications.

The area of curriculum renewal offers an important opportunity to include the gender dimension in the body of knowledge studied in various disciplines. If gender equality is a tenet of a nation's development agenda, then it can be a mainstream issue to be reflected in the educational curriculum at every level. At tertiary level, this is quite possible according to the female academics and professionals writing in *Women and the University Curriculum* (Holden Rønning and Kearney, 1996). A gender perspective can be included in the teaching of classical fields such as law, medicine, commerce, the humanities and the sciences, as well as in newer transdisciplinary domains, notably the environment and cultural studies. As a complement, certain groups advocate much stronger support for the teaching of gender studies as a way of advancing understanding of the main issues and their societal impact.

Curriculum reform that includes the gender dimension can achieve two objectives: on the one hand, it can sensitize a wider public to help foster attitudinal change; on the other hand, it illustrates the direct link between the curriculum and development issues, thus reinforcing the quest for relevance.

Lastly, the challenges facing universities are particularly stiff because of their centuries-old tradition of male-dominated culture in certain contexts. Elsewhere, in institutions where cloning has taken place, these tend to adhere strictly to replicating the original model. Nevertheless, change is inevitable, and truly enlightened university leadership will move rapidly and firmly to promote gender equality – in principle and in practice – to ensure that higher education plays its proper role in women's empowerment.

Conclusion: From Empowerment to Power-sharing

Engagement in civil society recalls our commitment to the habits of the heart.
Alexis De Toqueville

These words were quoted in a lecture given by Hillary Rodham Clinton at the Sorbonne during the summer of 1999. She was referring to the necessary interaction between government, the economy and civil society for the success of the development process in any country. She also stressed the predominance of women in the last area, likening this to De Toqueville's admiration for the commitment of ordinary people to civility, solidarity and neighbourliness. These are often described as the 'soft' values – viewed to some extent as 'feminine', and thus held in low esteem. Ms Clinton noted that, given the poor representation of women in governmental and economic positions, these values are bound to be absent, and therefore every effort should be made to redress this imbalance. The implication for women is that they must be ready to enter the arena of decision-making and to insist on codes of behaviour that reflect the concerns of society at large – namely, harmony as opposed to violence, fairness as opposed to corruption and advancement rather than deterrence.

As regards gender equality, women's empowerment can lead to power-sharing in the sense of full citizenship for men and women alike for the benefits of their communities. Empowerment must also embrace women's in-powerment, so the values they espouse can play an influential role in social decision-making. It must thus seek to eradicate – or at least neutralize – the pernicious traditional modes of in-powerment based on shifting, expedient alliances founded on force and self-interest.

Can cultural barriers be removed to create this new paradigm of social governance, which assures that women are empowered in the real sense of the term? And, can universities play an effective role in this process? The experiences recounted in this book give cause for cautious optimism:

1 *The relevance of universities for social development* is proved by the success of their programmes in fields such as basic education and community health and management, as Susan Van der Vynckt describes as happening in Africa and Maria D'Ávila Neto and Cíntia Simões Pires in Latin America. These programmes give people the life skills needed for effective citizenship, and thus empower the women who participate in them. Moreover, the benefits of higher education for women are advocated by Peter Katjavivi, who expresses strong support for enhancing women's access and participation as a major factor for social progress.

2 *The conceptual and cultural basis for gender equality* remains a complex domain, as the chapters by Abdalla Bubtana, Nina Arnhold and Ralitsa Muharska illustrate. The spiritual and religious foundations of certain cultures may affirm the equality of women, but these principles can also be interpreted to women's detriment by their male counterparts. In other contexts, the concepts of gender and of women's empowerment for their freedom of choice are slight, if not unknown – further time and support will be needed to foster the understanding and attitudinal support needed for their recognition. In addition, the issues of legitimacy of affirmative action and positive discrimination are discussed by Binod Khadria.

3 *Old and new paradigms of power in the academic management* are now in evidence, according to Dr Sheryl Bond, Anne Holden Rønning, Robyn Munford, Sylvia Rumball, Dr Berit Olsson and Professor Christina Ullenius. The old paradigm is male-dominated, and

perpetuates advancement based on mainly relational criteria; the new paradigm is less hierarchical, gender-neutral and oriented towards power-sharing for optimal results. Thus, both approaches must be better harmonized in academic management models of the future, including – crucially – the numbers of women in posts of influence.

Thus, the elements of the equation for women's empowerment and inpowerment are in place. But can they be correctly rebalanced to achieve full empowerment for women from all cultures? This constitutes a major social challenge for universities in the twenty-first century.

Bibliography

Bond, S. 1997. *Service and Self-respect: Women Leaders in Latin American Universities.* UNESCO.

Gibbons, M. 1998. *Higher Education Relevance in the 21st Century.* Washington D.C., World Bank.

Gleeson, J. (ed.) 1998. *EEO Case Studies: Good Practice Guidelines.* UNESCO.

Griffiths, S. (ed.) 1996. *Beyond the Glass Ceiling.* Manchester University Press.

Holden Rønning, A.; Kearney, M.-L. (eds), 1996. *Women and the University Curriculum.* London, Jessica Kingsley.

Kets De Vries, M. 1993. *Leaders, Fools and Imposters.* San Francisco, Jossey-Bass.

Nussbaum, M., Glover, J. (eds), 1995. *Women, Culture and Development.* Oxford, Clarendon Press.

OECD 1998. *Redefining Tertiary Education.* Paris, OECD.

Schmittroth, L. (ed.) 1995. *Statistical Record of Women Worldwide (2nd edn).* New York, Gale Research.

Smith, A.; Webster, F. (eds), 1997. *The Postmodern University.* London, SHRE/Open University Press.

UNDP. 1997, 1998, 1999. *The Human Development Report.* New York.

UNESCO/Commonwealth Secretariat. 1994. *Women and Higher Education Management.* Paris.

UNESCO. 1999. *Intergovernmental Conference on Cultural Policies for Development, Stockholm, 1998. (Final Report).* Paris.

———. 1998. *The World Education Report.* Paris.

———. 1996. *Our Cultural Diversity.* Paris.

———. 1998. *Women, Higher Education and Development: Issues and Perspectives.* Working Document for the Thematic Debate at the World Conference on Higher Education, Paris, 1998.

World Bank. 1998. *World Development Indicators.* Washington, D.C.

Part I

THE MEANING OF EMPOWERMENT

Chapter 1

GENDER-BASED POSITIVE DISCRIMINATION: IS THERE A CASE?

Binod Khadria

In the affirmative-action debate, one does not come across an adequate or intellectually satisfying defense of positive discrimination *favouring women over men* in education, employment and promotion to decision-making positions of power including those in politics. Surprisingly, the debate over the justification or legitimacy of positive-discrimination policies against non-discrimination is devoid of any such attempt. Whatever one usually comes across in this regard is too general, and does not make any distinction amongst the various target groups of positive-discrimination policies viz., ethnic, racial, religious, sexual (i.e., gender-based)[1] etc., or between one and the rest. In trying to answer the title question, therefore, this chapter makes an important departure from the trend. The underlying purpose is to convince other men (i.e., apart from myself) and all women that positive discrimination in favour of women (including girls, over men and boys) as the disadvantaged target group yields results that are unique when compared with the outcomes of positive discrimination targeted at other groups. This chapter also finds a unique justification for this in pointing out *family* as a cultural or institutional entity separate from *community* within society, where the traditional discrimination that calls for positive discrimination originated in the first place. This chapter thus contributes to the ongoing debate on the legitimacy of positive discrimination in favour of women.

---

1. The terms 'sexual' or 'gender-based' have been used interchangeably here without implying any bias in connotation. Similarly, at times 'men'/'women' and 'male'/'female' have been used interchangeably without any prejudice whatsoever.

Positive discrimination, affirmative action, reverse discrimination, etc., are some of the terms used interchangeably for referring to the policies of preferential treatment given to specifically identified target group(s). Such policies are practised while giving admissions into educational institutions, recruiting in the labour market, promoting employees to decision-making positions within public- and private-sector organizations, and while power-sharing in politics. This is done with the purpose of equalizing opportunities so as to counteract the historical or traditional discrimination that took place in the past against such groups. As mentioned earlier, such target groups are generally racial, ethnic and sexual, but those based on other ascribable personal characteristics, such as religious, caste-oriented or lin-guistic minority groups, are also found in particular societies or countries.

Although the most practised or discussed programme of positive discrim-ination is one based on numerical quota(s) or 'reservation(s)' in admissions, employment, promotion and so on, there is a range of rules that are being considered in applying the principle to practice. Drawing from the list of Sumner (1987), these rules may be restated as: (1) *special drive*, where target groups are informed of the openings (in education as well as jobs) and encouraged to apply for them; (2) *tie-breaking*, where target-group appli-cants are preferred to equally qualified non-target-group applicants; (3) *handicapping*, whereby target-group applicants are given preference over bet-ter qualified non-target-group applicants; (4) *lexical assessment*, which ignores non-target applicants altogether unless there is no suitably qualified target group applicant; and (5) *numerical goals or quotas*, whereby stipulated num-bers or proportions of target-group members are inducted in educational and work places. Sometimes a combination of these rules is also applied. In India, for example, quotas exist for socially deprived groups called Scheduled Castes (SCs), Scheduled Tribes (STs) and Other Backward Castes (OBCs) in admissions to higher-education institutions. In employment too, there are constitutional requirements for fulfilling quotas for these groups. In both cases, special drives are often also undertaken. There are no religious or women's quotas in India so far, although special efforts are now being made to encourage girls and women to participate in education and the labour market. The latest, of course, is the Women's Reservation Bill for creating a quota of 33 per cent of seats in the Indian Parliament's lower house and in the state assemblies.[2] The enactment of the bill has, however, remained stalled for well over a year now because of the demands and dismissals of the claims to separate sub-reservations for *all the other* minority/disadvantaged categories of women, rather than women as one single disadvantaged group.

The issue of preferential treatment for disadvantaged group(s) is thus a complex one. Unfortunately, as stated earlier, only an omnibus approach has

2. See *Times of India* (1997) for some details of the debate, which is still ongoing.

been followed so far in arguing the case for or against the use of preferential treatment (through quotas for example) – be it in the case of the Blacks or the Jews in America; the Scheduled Castes (SCs), Scheduled Tribes (STs) or Other Backward Castes (OBCs) in India; or women in all countries the world over. No attempt has been made to analyse whether these different groups vary from each other, or whether one group differs from the rest in terms of either the justification or the implications of positive discrimination. Notwithstanding this lacuna, a sample survey of the rationales erected both in support of and against positive discrimination, becomes imperative as a principle of public policy. This must precede any attempt at making a separate case for preferential treatment to women through positive discrimination (whether in education, employment, or any kind of power-sharing) in any society. I have, therefore, selected the following two pieces of literature on the subject to draw my samples of the rationales from – one each to represent the sides against and for positive discrimination respectively.

Let me first put forth the case *against* positive discrimination. The most telling reason for such a case lies in the American principle of antidiscrimination in employment. This principle of antidiscrimination, as Loury (1987) points out, 'has a noble intellectual pedigree, harking back to the Enlightenment-era challenge to *hereditary authority*' (p. 252, author's italics). According to Loury, though the recalcitrant persistence of group disparity in the face of formal equality of opportunity has forced many liberals to look to race-conscious public action as the only viable remedy, it is still true that the institution of group-conscious policy implicitly confers special *public status* on the historic injustices faced by its beneficiary groups and hence devalues, implicitly, the injustices endured by others.

On the other side of the story, although an apparently strong case seems to have been cast for preferential treatment of women, the arguments are equally applicable to any other group(s) vying for similar preference or preferences. Sumner (1987), in putting forth the case, says, 'discriminatory hiring practices remain an important barrier in the path of working women and thus an important factor in the oppression of all women' (p. 215). According to him, 'this provides a strong case for its [a quota system's] implementation' (p. 215). He further adds that women, comprising on the average between one-quarter and one-half of the national labour force in many countries, tend to be clustered in employment sectors – especially clerical, sales and service occupations – that rank relatively low in remuneration, status, autonomy and other perquisites, leaving the more prestigious and rewarding managerial and professional positions, as well as the major categories of blue-collar jobs, largely to the male preserve. While conceding that such a widespread and persistent pattern has many roots, Sumner stresses that all the unexplained reasons can be attributed to discriminatory practices on the part of the employers.

Both the authors cited above as belonging to two different camps – one cautious in recommending outright support for preferential policy of positive discrimination as the only or the best, and the other extending unqualified support to 'sexual positivism' – have, however, a common ground in looking to discriminatory public policies to be either corrective or consequentialist (Loury uses the terms 'enforcement-oriented' and 'result-oriented', respectively). Whereas both denounce the former as based on either a *quid pro quo* or a tit-for-tat principle of compensation for historical discrimination, Loury laments that the distinction remains largely obscured by the supporters of race-conscious policy of affirmative action. While my own vote for policies of positive discrimination in favour of women is triggered largely by my faith in their result-oriented or consequentialist (also 'prospective' or 'distributive' in the language of Sumner) outcomes, my justification takes into account the *quid pro quo* or the so-called corrective perspective as well: if we trace back the cause of gender discrimination to its deepest roots, then I would like to emphasize that it originates not so much *in* the labour market where, as Sumner says, the employers play the role of agents, but outside of it – within the family itself, where women and men are (and *were,* historically) given unequal treatments. This, to my mind, is unique to the history of gender discrimination, because for all other disadvantaged groups the discrimination originates not in the family, but out in the community or society of which the labour market forms an integral part. This is a crucial distinction between the gender (or the sexual) discrimination on the one hand, and all the other types of group discriminations on the other. Unfortunately, this important distinction has neither been noted nor focused upon in the deliberations on preferential treatment. What follows from this distinction is an acceptable relevance of the corrective perspective of *quid pro quo*, but let me first elaborate on the consequentialist or distributive advantage of a gender-based positive discrimination.

As a result-oriented or consequentialist policy intervention by the state, the outcomes of a gender-based positive discrimination are likely to be different from those targeted at any or all other disadvantaged groups, viz., those based on racial, ethnic, linguistic, religious or caste considerations. Firstly, if *some* individuals (women only) in *all* families are the recipients of protection rather than *all* individuals (both women and men) of *all* families in *some* communities only (which are then the recipients in the latter case), the benefits of the former get distributed over the entire canvas of that society where it is applied. This happens because of the unique distribution of its womenfolk across each and every family[3] – as mothers, sisters, wives

3. Excepting, of course, (a) the unusual gay families (which also may be taken care of by adoption of a female child) but including the lesbian ones; and (b) the eunuchs, where the concept of a family usually does not exist (as in India where the community overtakes) – both types, however, being in minuscule proportions in society.

and/or daughters will transmit the benefits *horizontally* to the male members as well, either directly or indirectly. When positive-discrimination policy is based on any other type of group characteristic (racial, ethnic and so on), only a section of society stands to benefit because the gains flow down a *vertical structure* of communities in social hierarchy, and tend to remain concentrated in few families where each and every member (both male and female) is eligible for receiving affirmative-action benefits. Since no explicit cognizance is taken of the possibility of benefits being transmitted from one member to another or from some to all through horizontal or quasi-horizontal structures within the family in such policy arrangements, there is the possibility that the benefits will be duplicated among some families, leaving others with none.

Secondly, the binomial distinction between men and women being biologically determined and nonreversible in nature (excepting through surgical and medical intervention), the susceptibility to manipulation in the distribution of benefits of a gender-based positive discrimination is minimal. In the other cases of positive discrimination based on racial, ethnic, religious, linguistic or caste identities of groups of people, manipulation through false certification and other corrupt means is less likely to be detected when compared with certification/identification of a person either as man or woman. This is important in an overpopulated country such as India or other poor countries, where the possibility of leakage of benefits of public policies to undeserving quarters through outright corruption, ineffective enforcement and unclear definitions of target categories is rather high. One may cite the example of a premier university in India during the early 1980s, where a highly commendable policy of admission based on a positive discrimination principle had to be diluted, and was eventually abandoned because of large scale manufacturing of fake caste and parental-income certificates that was taking place in the campus itself (*see* Khadria, 1998a). Similarly, one may think of the public outrage against the implementation of the Mandal Commission's recommendations for large-scale caste-based reservations in government jobs in the late 1980s.

Coming back to the corrective or 'enforcement-oriented' objective of *quid pro quo*, positive discrimination based on gender difference has an advantage over the other types on this count, too. In the former case, it is possible that the very same families that had experienced gender discrimination in an earlier generation will gain in later generation(s) if positive discrimination is targeted towards women. In the case of other types, such a possibility is likely to get thwarted by the probability of the preferential-treatment benefits going (and continuing to go) to the already well-off families, rather than to those that had undergone sufferings in the past and have continued to remain deprived. When one goes wrong in this regard, whereas in the women's case the damage is likely to be limited to a proportion of roughly one-half only (following the proportion of women and girls in the population in most countries) (*see* Raju et al., 1999), the extent of damage remains undetermined in the other types precisely because of the complex nature of the identification and measurement of upward socioeconomic mobility. This brings in the question of priority of equality *between groups* over equality *within groups*. In this context, Loury (1987, p. 250) raises the question: 'Why is inequality among individuals of the same group acceptable when inequality between the groups is not?' Loury interprets this to be the usually unanswered question of 'why the *ethnic-racial-sexual* identification of "group" should take precedence over all others', and concludes, 'it is a question usually avoided in popular discussions of the need to equalize group disparities' (p. 250). Contrary to this assertion, the corrective perspective of gender-based affirmative action provides us with a rationale to state that *sexual* identification of the group can be granted, if at all, a precedence over the *ethnic-racial* (and other types of) identifications. It is because of this precedence that gender classification can be used as a *necessary condition* even where positive discrimination is introduced and administered for the benefit of the other disadvantaged group or groups, leaving their identification as only a *sufficient condition* for receiving the benefits on consequentialist grounds. Even when the dilemma cannot be got over completely this way, there are ways to resolve the conflict between personal interests of two different groups of individuals on the one hand, or between personal interest and public judgement of a given group or individual while targeting the benefits of a positive-discrimination policy (*see* Majumdar, 1980, and an elaboration of the mechanism in Khadria, 1998b). Without going into the details of that mechanism here, it may still be called a smart and wise decision to distinguish between families (rather than communities) deserving the protection of positive discrimination and those not deserving it by classifying the status of womenfolk in society as a proxy variable, instead of comparing the various skin colours, or faiths, beliefs, customs, languages, incomes and so on of different communities.

To sum up, in an important departure from the trend in the literature, I have, in this chapter, presented only one argument: gender-based positive discrimination in favour of women is distinctly different from those based on other group characteristics – to the extent that it needs to be weighed on a different scale than the rest. This, however, need not mean that positive discrimination for all other groups is bad and to be avoided. Even where society puts its priority on egalitarianism through emancipation of the other groups, gender-based positive discrimination can be used as a strategic route to achieve that goal. I have, however, presented a distinctive justification for casting one's vote in support of gender-based discrimination in favour of women in its own right, even in the extreme case of a nonbeliever discarding positive discrimination as a principled tool of state intervention in the first place. My presumption is that one does not come across such justification in the literature readily available on the subject of equality and inequality. If this is true, then I consider this chapter to have made at least one positive contribution to the whole debate on positive discrimination, and that contribution stands for the cause of women. Therefore, I advise the readers to move on to the discussion of other substantial issues, such as what I would qualify as 'effective' access, 'curricular' awareness, and 'operational' empowerment of women in matters of education, employment and promotion to decision-making positions[4], with greater confidence. If not, I shall urge them to consider it just as an important reminder and a rejuvenator.

Bibliography

Khadria, B. 1998a. 'JNU Mechanism for Monitoring Egalitarian Policies', *Journal of Higher Education*, Vol. 21, No.1, pp.101-15.
———. 1998b. 'The Societal Agenda for Women in Higher Education', paper presented in the Thematic Debate on Women and Higher Education at the *World Conference on Higher Education*, mimeo., UNESCO, Paris.
Loury, G.C. 1987. 'Why Should We Care About Group Inequality?' In: E. Frankel Paul, F.D. Miller Jr., J. Paul and J. Ahrens (eds), *Equal Opportunity*, Oxford, Basil Blackwell.
Majumdar, T. 1980. 'Rationality of Changing Choice', *Analyse and Kritik*, Vol. 2, No. 2, pp. 172-8.
Raju, S.; Atkins, P.J.; Kumar, N.; Townsend, J.G. 1999. *Atlas of Women and Men in India*, New Delhi, Kali for Women.
Sumner, L.W. 1987. 'Positive Sexism'. In: E. F. Paul et al. (eds). *Equal Opportunity*, Oxford, Basil Blackwell.
'Political Patriarchy: Reservation About Power for Women', *Times of India* (New Delhi), 24 May 1997.

4. I have elaborated upon these issues elsewhere (*see* Khadria, 1998a). Sumner (1987, pp. 214–5) also talks of such qualifications in terms of 'a variety of complimentary measures', like day-care facilities, flexible and part-time working hours, protection against sexual harassment in the workplace and so on.

Chapter 2

WOMEN GRADUATES IN THE FORMER GDR: TOWARDS EMPOWERMENT

Nina Arnhold

Introduction

This short chapter examines some aspects of the situation of women in the German Democratic Republic before 1989 and during the transition process, focusing to some extent on woman in academia. Despite declarations claiming the contrary, women in the German Democratic Republic had to come to terms with a double work-load, as the overwhelming majority worked full-time and also carried out most of the housework. Despite state-socialist propaganda claiming that the socialist state would realize the full participation of women in every part of society, the number of female professors and leaders in society was not substantially higher than in most Western countries. Feminist concepts, which might have helped to analyse the situation, were rarely known and were not publicly discussed. The events of 1989 and the German unification process led to a transition period in which women in Eastern Germany have had to redefine their roles and aims.

Conditions of Women in Eastern Germany before 1989

On the surface, a gender problem did not exist, as the equality of men and women was ensured by legislation. The family law proclaimed a new type of relationship between men and women in which the spouses had the responsibility to create a relationship that allowed both of them to develop their abilities and talents fully for their own good and the wider good of society.

Officially, women were encouraged to participate in all areas of public life, and they were expected to work. Indeed, about half of the work-force and half of students at higher-education institutions, in vocational training or in upper secondary schools were female (Helwig, 1988). The underlying political assumption of this policy was provided by the Marxist-Leninist ideology that the participation in the process of production must be the key factor in the development and self-fulfilment of the socialist personality. However, it should also be noted that there has always been a shortage of employees in the German Democratic Republic.

Certain tendencies indicate that women found it difficult to fulfil their tasks at the work place as well as their tasks in the family. The birth rate decreased while the number of divorces increased substantially during the 1970s and the 1980s. More and more women with children chose part-time work. The state attempted to counteract these tendencies by a number of socio-political measures: the further improvement of child care facilities, interest-free credit for young families and other forms of financial support for mothers (including single mothers).

As Helwig (1988) has pointed out, these measures led instead to the perpetuation of the old role models, as their focus continued to be the mother of the child. Instead, it would have been more desirable to encourage men and women to share housework and the responsibility for the upbringing of children. Crèches, kindergarten and after-school facilities were free and available to all. This impressive provision of free child-care facilities should be seen as a rather ambiguous phenomenon, in that it allowed women to work full-time, but it also enabled the state to have a strong impact on the development of the child, i.e., to support the formation of socialist personalities.

Higher Education and Female Leadership before 1989

As mentioned above, a gender problem did not officially exist. On the other hand, the actual percentage of leaders who were female looked, in a number of areas, as depressing as those for most Western countries. The official numbers indicate that, in agriculture and industry, only one in five, and in the state administration, only one in four executive positions was held by a woman (Helwig, 1988). There were rarely any female political leaders, and just one female minister – Margot Honecker, education minister and wife of the state and party leader Erich Honecker.

The situation is similar as far as higher education is concerned. In the German Democratic Republic, women were encouraged to choose untypical subjects, such as the engineering sciences. This choice was supported by a strong limitation on the numbers of students, especially in the social sciences and humanities, and via entrance examinations. The attitude towards the socialist state also played an important role in this context. But as one looks at the hierarchy within higher education, one sees the same underrepresentation of women in terms of professorships. In higher education, women made up 9.1 per cent of high-ranking academic teachers and 37 per cent of the *Mittelbau*, the medium-level academic teachers (Felber and Baume, 1997). Many women remained in the *Mittelbau*, which was, in many cases, more engaged with teaching than with research. While it seems that this form of employment allowed many women to combine their different interests and duties, at the same time, it is evident that many factors that had traditionally hindered female careers and leadership continued to have an impact in the socialist countries of Eastern and Central Europe. Female leadership as a distinctive concept might have been considered and executed by some individuals but, publicly, such a concept has not been discussed.

Problems of Transition

The transformation of higher education in Eastern Germany during the course of unification as well as the education system in general, turned out to be a process of adjustment to the structure of the West (Weiler et al.; Simon, 1995). The implementation of a system in the East, which was completely different from the prevailing system, caused a number of problems. Numerous subjects and institutions were *abgewickelt*, or liquidated, mainly because they were perceived as close to the system and the Marxist-Leninist ideology. This applied rather to the social sciences and humanities than to the traditionally male-dominated subjects. At the Humboldt-Universität in former East Berlin for example, 90 per cent of the professors in mathematics kept their jobs compared to 10 per cent in pedagogical sciences. After some form of political evaluation, Eastern German academics could apply for their own posts. In many cases, academics from the West were appointed. The so-called *Mittelbau*, which was, in the old German Democratic Republic, considered similar to a profession, was reduced drastically in order to fit with the Western German model.

The personnel of higher-education institutions in Eastern Germany of 1989 (30,945) was reduced by half (16,458). The *Mittelbau* was reduced by about 60 per cent. For the remaining jobs, a thorough mix of academics from East and the West was envisaged. For the Humboldt-Universität, this led to the following composition (without medicine): out of all C4 professors (the highest rank out of three types of professorships), 67 per cent come from West Germany and 33 per cent from Eastern Germany. Out of 100 per cent C4 professors, 5 per cent are women from the West and 3 per cent are women from the East; 53 per cent of the C3 professors come from the former German Democratic Republic, and 22 per cent of all C3 professors are women. The total percentage of female professors at the Humboldt-Universität is 12 per cent, 4 per cent less than in 1989, but substantially more than the average in the united Federal Republic of Germany (Felber and Baume, 1997).

In principle, unemployment was an unknown phenomenon in the German Democratic Republic. After 1989, however, women were often the first to lose their jobs. For the personal situation of the women concerned, it meant that, in many cases, women had to rediscover role models that had been – at least on the surface – long forgotten.

A reorientation of women in Eastern Germany is deeply desirable, but rather difficult. Ralitsa Muharska (1996) has shown in her research activity on the introduction of women's studies in Bulgarian universities how feminism is perceived by women in Bulgaria: as something imported from the West, which possibly creates new divisions in an already deeply divided society. The same negative attitude towards feminism appears prevalent among many women in Eastern Germany. There is a reluctance to consider new models that might help to analyse the current situation. In this, as in so many other respects, the transition period still continues. The implementation of new structures seems easy in comparison with the problem of changing attitudes and creating a civil society that fills the newly established institutions with new thinking.

Bibliography

Felber, C.; Baume, B. 1997. 'Karrierechancen, aufhaltsamer oder aushaltsamer Abstieg? Wissenschaftlerinnen aus Ost und West im Interview'. In: H. Macha and M. Klinkhammer (eds), *Die andere Wissenschaft: Stimmen der Frauen an Hochschulen.* Bielefeld, Kleine Verlag.

Helwig, G. 1988. 'Frauen und Familie'. In: A. Fischer (ed.). *Ploetz: Die Deutsche Demokratische Republik. Daten, Fakten, Analysen.* Darmstadt, Wissenschaftliche Buchgesellschaft.

Muharska, R. 1996. 'Women's Studies in Bulgarian Universities: A Success Story?' In: M.-L. Kearney and A. Holden Rønning (eds). *Women and the University Curriculum: Towards Equality, Democracy and Peace.* London/Paris, Jessica Kingsley/UNESCO Publishing.

Simon, D. 1995. 'Verschludert und verschleudert', *Die Zeit,* Vol. 7, No. 4.

Weiler, H.N. et al. 1995. *Educational Change and Social Transformation: Teachers, Schools and Universities in Eastern Germany.* London, Falmer Press.

Chapter 3

THE CONCEPT OF EMPOWERMENT: A CULTURAL ISSUE

Ralitsa Muharska

One would say that improving the present situation of women in higher education is one of those issues that clearly needs immediate action on the part of the entire academic establishment. But, in reality, the people who are actually most likely to *do* something about it are, in my opinion, those involved with the functioning of centres and departments for women's and gender studies. These academically based entities serve as an important gender-sensitizing force in their immediately surrounding communities, as well as in their societies. Certainly, this is the case for societies outside the West, where gender sensitivity is practically unknown.

For such centres and departments, the adequate representation of women in both the student and academic bodies, as well as the defense of their interests, is not only a matter of political concern, but also an issue of professional interest. Thus, the dual motivation involved should not be underestimated. It is from those who are most involved and motivated that initiatives and action can be expected – at least, they can be relied on never to let the university leadership forget or close their eyes to problems of gender equity. Yet, all too often, the position of such centres is academically marginal, even in countries with decades of tradition in both gender studies and democratic pluralism. There are several reasons for this, most of which are political. Despite these facts, what I think these centres need most – and, fortunately, receive in many instances – are powerful networks of support on the international level.

By way of example, I should like to share my experience in setting up such a centre and keeping it afloat during the last seven years. This experience, to my best knowledge, is rather typical of what has been happening lately in many parts of the world, the so-called 'countries-in-transition', places as diverse as the former Soviet republics of Central Asia, South Africa, Haiti, the Balkans, and Eastern and Central Europe. They could, therefore, be considered both representative and indicative of current trends that are important.

Before 1990, there was, of course, nothing like these centres in these parts of the world. So everything had to start from scratch, relying on little expertise and practically no funding, but great enthusiasm. In fact, these centres were set up precisely because it became necessary to overcome the conservatism and resistance of the academic establishment. This was the case at Sofia University in Bulgaria (as well as in all neighbouring countries), since non-governmental organizations (NGOs), which were rather loosely affiliated to the university, gave these centres independence, helped them with the problem of fundraising in a foundering economy and promoted their academic credibility. It also made them, in a natural way, part of the restored – or, newly emerging – democracy after years of totalitarianism, during which the women's movement in the respective countries had done little to promote or improve gender awareness. In fact, communism had declared women's equality on paper, but the reality was quite different. Women themselves were tired of that hypocrisy and their double burden.

Thus, without the support (financial, methodological and personal) from already-existing institutions of this type (mainly in the West), as well as international organizations (the International Federation of University Women in our case) and foundations, both governmental and private, creating these centres for gender studies would have been impossible. As of 1998, there are now such centres or departments in over thirty countries, and in probably at least twice as many universities where Gender Studies had been unheard of until a few years ago.

As a result, it will be more difficult for leaders (academic or in other areas) in these contexts to disregard problems of gender equity in academia or in society at large. In my view, what really empowers these centres is the fact that they are linked together in a recently established network (thanks to the Open Society Fund). Thus, experience can be shared (and I, for one, can testify how necessary this is when you are at first base wondering which way to go), efforts can be directed well and efficiency significantly increased.

This, I believe, is the important role of international structures, particularly those in the United Nations system: namely, to establish and support such networks on a global scale, and not just at the regional level. I am convinced that this could be a worthwhile and workable UNESCO strategy for future action to further enhance gender equality in higher education, as it seems to be in keeping with the general goals and policies adopted by this Organization. Indeed, one could hardly over-emphasize its positive impact, especially since it need not be very costly.

Chapter 4

EMPOWERING WOMEN IN BUSINESS AND THE PROFESSIONS: A QUESTION OF SKILLS

Sylvia Perry

Introduction

At the end of the twentieth century, we witness the reality of a critical mass of women in the global labour market. However, although women constitute a major force, their importance is not fully recognized. Their absence from decision-making in the economic and productive sectors is a glaring example of their inequality, and one of the areas identified to be remedied by the Beijing Platform for Action.

Today, more women work in the business and professional fields. Yet, their preparation for these and their actual performance can be explained by quite different orientations. On the one hand, business covers a wide range of activities for which education may – or may not – be a pre-requisite. On the other hand, women have entered the professions in far greater numbers, largely because of their greatly increased access to higher education. This includes their presence in commercial and economic fields where academic qualifications are required. Globally, women are generally better represented in the professional and technical category than in administrative and managerial positions.

It is clear that women who succeed in these domains are empowered, and therefore able to achieve many objectives related to their personal and working lives. However, I perceive that women in business and those in the professions (such as medicine, law and engineering) must deal with quite different contexts. This has special significance when their performance in varied cultural environments is examined – here, the term 'culture' can refer either to their geographical location or to the specific milieu in which they work. Related questions are the type of skills required for each activity and the role of education in their acquisition.

The International Federation of Business and Professional Women (IFBPW), which has more than 100 national associations in all regions of the world, is a non-governmental organization (NGO) whose members have extremely diverse profiles and backgrounds. For this reason, the IFBPW is well placed to comment on the issue of women's empowerment in relation to cultural contexts and to suggest how higher education institutions, including universities, may contribute to equipping women with the skills required for their future working lives.

Women in the Work-force

For the past two decades, the volatile state of global employment has been a source of major concern for all countries, whether rich or poor. The root causes of these problems are complex and involve:

- the long-term consequences of population growth and urbanization;
- uneven and destabilizing patterns in the world's economic growth;
- structural issues, such as depressed manufacturing sectors in many countries, the rise of service industries, the fluctuating state of certain Asian economies, and the impact of the difficulties of transition to market systems in Central and Eastern European countries;
- significant rapid technological developments affecting work patterns and the stability of labour forces; and
- the internationalization of the labour market.

The place of women in this changing context is of particular interest. According to the *World Development Indicators*, women constitute between 26 per cent and 44 per cent of national work-forces worldwide (the Muslim countries of the Middle East, sub-Saharan Africa and Southern Asia relate to the lower ratio).

Furthermore, the numbers of women exceed those of men in the following:

Table 4.1. *National work-forces worldwide by area and sex*

Area	Women	Men
Agricultural	52%	48%
Service	32%	29%
Industry	15%	23%

Source: *World Development Indicators*, 1998

However, one of the fastest-growing categories for women in both the developed and the developing countries of the world is that of self-employment and entrepreneurship, but even so there is great variance among different countries.

Various sources show that in Europe, every third new business is created by a woman; some 18 million women in total are engaged in an entrepreneurial activity, roughly 20 per cent of Europe's labour force. In Canada, women have been starting their own businesses at three times the rate of men. Women in the U.S.A. own approximately 40 per cent of all American businesses, and the same percentage is the representation of women in Australian business ownership. In India, women entrepreneurs make up 20 per cent of the total entrepreneurs, and even in Japan, 24 per cent of business owners are women.

In addition, we must consider that women often work part-time, are paid less than men for the same work, and are very underrepresented at the management levels of their occupations. Women who work in the business and professional fields figure in all these parameters. Important variables affecting women are their roles in different cultural contexts, levels of empowerment, and the value of education and training.

Cultural Contexts in Business and the Professions

Today, culture and context can be interchangeable concepts. A range of these can be observed across our understanding of the global society. Firstly, context can be defined as geographical, where region, race and the predominance of one or several cultures are key aspects. Secondly, they can be seen from a perspective where industrialized countries enjoy conditions that differ both from countries-in-transition and from those in the developing world. Thirdly, the psychological aspects can gain importance as we define a context or a culture from the point of view of its dominant actors and their attitudes or thinking.

As a result, it is possible to consider the Western standard of living as a culture of materialism. From this, it becomes easy to describe specific 'niches' in society as cultures – for example, those of academic life and of each profession. The business world has created its own culture, but this is particularly varied in its manifestations and in the profiles of its inhabitants.

It goes without saying that each of these contexts – or cultures – views the gender issue in its own light and according to criteria resulting from the history and conduct of each culture. Women who are active in business or professional life constitute a specific focus group and, as such, they are located in relation to these criteria, which are themselves evolving and reacting to a changing world.

As economic agents, women are familiar figures in virtually all contexts and cultures, often combining this activity with their roles as spouses and mothers. For women in traditional and family businesses, brought up in a culture where education and training have been geared to the variable requirements of the enterprise, they have been well accepted as partners and co-workers.

For professional and graduate women, the cultural context is not the same. Higher education has been the traditional training ground for social and economic leaders. So, such qualifications have permitted women to enter the ruling elite, albeit in small numbers, and to address the priority issues of national development. In former times, such women were few, and so were concerned with the power politics of governance. Nowadays, development is a complex goal for rich and poor countries alike, and thus problems must be addressed more practically. In this regard, much larger numbers of women graduates in the professions can bring about a sea change in prevailing attitudes to authority, to responsibility and to problem-solving.

As many more women have now gained access to higher learning, they are gradually entering fields previously dominated by men. This is true of the academic disciplines of business studies, commerce and economics, which have traditionally been very dominated by male students and described as 'gender-insensitive' in terms of content. In *Women and the University Curriculum* (1996), Gardner and King prefer to describe this situation as being 'gender blind' since it results from a dominant male paradigm that is unchallenged and hence remains the norm. Such contexts are frequently modelled on Western culture, and thus the importance of material success in a global economic environment is stressed.

Despite such limitations, these disciplines have proved attractive everywhere, and more recently, even in countries in transition such as Bulgaria and Romania, which have witnessed huge demands for these fields of study.

But it can be forgotten that these professional environments are usually tough. Until now, in order to advance (and even to survive), women had to learn the male rules of the game in order to carve out a career. Indeed, it can be argued that these cultures (now so globally evident) have embraced women who play by the old man-made rules. When, at the same time, women have elected to raise families, it is not surprising that they have found themselves facing conditions of dual stress on the professional and personal fronts.

But as employment grows volatile, women (and even some men) are reacting against the male-dominated professional environments. More emphasis is placed on flexibility, quality time and personal satisfaction through creative work – for this, entrepreneurial skills are needed to adapt to very different styles of life and work.

In contrast, business people everywhere have been and still are a different and more varied breed. Where there has been a lack of academic training, this in no way impedes their natural acumen to sell and trade. They progress thanks to their practical skills and ability to adapt. This situation is particularly interesting with regard to women from the developing world. Women are very often part of the economic livelihood of the family – they work on the family farm, run market stalls or manage small enterprises. They not only work alongside men – fathers, husbands and sons – on an equal basis, but, in increasing circumstances where women are heading up families they are also being recognized for their emerging competitiveness and independence. In contrast, their 'corporate sisters', even with the benefits of greater education, are still facing the same 'old-boy-network' barriers as their counterparts in truly professional fields. Ironically, while some women in developing and poor countries who are economically active enjoy certain advantages of attitude and acceptance, not all traditional cultures will recognize successful women in business as rightful leaders.

As one might expect, this complex background of culture and context has a clear impact on the level and nature of business and professional women's empowerment.

Empowerment: Education and Skills

Empowerment can be defined as the ability to acquire the capacity to manage one's own life and to have the confidence to realize one's goals, whether this means shedding the burden of poverty in the developing world, or succeeding in balancing the constraints of one's personal and working life in the financially adequate or upper social echelons of countries (either rich or poor) worldwide.

Education is widely considered to be the main source of empowerment, and is a force that can bring vital results for women. For this reason, today all governments are committed to improving female enrolments at all levels of education. In poor countries, however, women's access to basic education is a top goal because of the positive contribution to development objectives, while the benefits of higher education are less apparent – especially if this subsector is limited to the purely academic sphere.

Thus, while not reducing the importance of education, it is essential to recall that empowerment means the acquisition of skills as well as knowledge and expertise. By way of example, skills associated with the business world can often be more useful than purely intellectual and analytic abilities. Today, much emphasis is placed on skill-based learning: communication skills, team work, adaptability, resilience, problem-solving, honing good judgement and negotiation. It is essential that business people acquire and use these skills from an early age and in practical contexts.

With regard to higher education, while this opens good prospects for women graduates, (despite current unemployment volatility, e.g., in Korea less than 30 per cent of college-educated women are employed, and those who are employed tend to occupy marginal jobs) the value of practical skills cannot be underestimated. Certainly, empowerment is not just an academic matter. Many of the capacities required can be learnt from a more interactive and society-orientated approach to education and training – and one which puts great value on practical experience.

Dr Monique Siegel, of the Swiss Federation of Business and Professional Women, has undertaken research on women in developing countries whose energy, industriousness and flair for identifying potential markets have resulted in their success as micro-entrepreneurs and business owners. Here, skills – rather than formal education are the essential factors.

However, having made the distinction of the various basic approaches to 'business' and 'professional' environments, there must be recognition that the two distinct categories (as previously recognized) of employment and social application are, in the global environment of today, required to have the attributes of the other. More and more, success in the corporate business world requires a sound higher-educational background, while economic forces press the academic institutions into a more market-orientated attitude. In whatever sphere of life, everyone has to recognize the 'bottom line' to ensure commercial viability.

Challenges for Universities

Today, in confirmation of the outcomes of the World Conference on Higher Education, it is agreed that universities must change to become more relevant and to be perceived as genuine partners in the development process. In so doing, they become part of the wider movement of post-secondary or tertiary education reform that seeks to equip learners of all ages for their social and professional roles in the world of the next millennium.

For this reason, academic skills must be balanced by those relevant to business – both are needed, and universities should interact more often with the community to foster the application of skills and to develop the range of competences needed by students preparing for their futures.

The world of business can and must develop closer links with higher-education institutions, as this is part of the current drive to enhance the relevance of higher education and illustrates that both sectors are working – in their respective ways – for social development.

The debate on the balance between education and skills should stress the importance of ethics in the teaching of academic disciplines related to this field. At a round-table held in Paris in 1998 on Business Ethics, which was co-sponsored by UNESCO and the International Association of Students in Economics and Management, the question of ethics was considered, drawing a distinction between codes of conduct in specific fields of professional life, such as medicine, law and genetics. It was concluded that, since the economy is a key motor of development and thus of global governance, higher education must place due emphasis on teaching business ethics and relating this subject to relevant aspects of globalization. The move to renovate the international financial architecture of loan schemes and debt repayments so as to permit countries to emerge from present impossible conditions of poverty is a good example. However, none of this can be achieved unless there is solid dialogue amongst the stakeholders in higher education and their counterparts in business and society. Thus, learning becomes an interactive experience.

Women are a key force in both business and professional environments. Because of their natural skills for conciliation and negotiation – honed by personal and domestic experience – they can uphold and inculcate values for a more equitable and human society. Their innate traits can be brought to the areas of social and business leadership, thus dismissing the compulsion to ape male stereotypes.

A perfect example of such feminine skills in leadership is Maria Doolan, head-hunted for the job of general manager of the member services of one of Australia's largest financial institutions. She started as a shop assistant, but now reports directly to her CEO. Her strategy of developing interpersonal skills, setting herself tough targets (including the acquisition of professional qualifications through distance learning), overcoming male attitudes and, most of all, 'never becoming one of the boys' by being confident to play by her own rules, was the means to her success.

Business and professional women have a unique wealth of experience, which must be passed to younger women who are seeking their career paths and personal lifestyles. In this regard, the advocacy and mentoring role of NGOs such as the IFBPW has evolved greatly in recent years.

The ultimate aim is women's empowerment, despite the range of cultural barriers – geographical or attitudinal – that impede this. Such empowerment must be interpreted broadly so as to permit women to realize their capacities, whatever their specific situation. For this reason, gender must be a cornerstone of higher education and institutional development – a bold step, still in its infancy.

Conclusion

From the IFBPW perspective, clearly the current trends in higher education and in the gender debate are of interest because they touch the lives and experiences of many of our members. However, the IFBPW is also uniquely placed to promote enhanced social and economic partnerships for higher education as a prime strategy for the renewal of its relevance.

This was the philosophy of the visionary IFBPW founder, Lena Madesin Phillips, who foresaw the very vital contribution to be made to social development by highly skilled women in all fields of human endeavour.

Part II

REGIONAL EXPERIENCES

Chapter 5

WOMEN, CULTURE AND POWER-SHARING: THE CASE OF THE ARAB REGION

Abdalla Bubtana

Introduction

Too many misconceptions concerning the status of women in the Arab region have prevailed during the last half of this century. All of these focused on the cultural and social dimensions, which, for most people, constitute major factors that prevent Arab women from reaching self-fulfilment. They therefore remain powerless, and only make marginal contributions to decision-making in all areas of society.

Although all Arab states share a common culture, as well as common values and traditions, the status of women and the level of empowerment they enjoy differ from one country to another. In some, women are highly involved in social and political decision-making, while in others, they do not yet have the right to stand for elections or even to cast their votes in these.

This situation can be interpreted in two ways. Firstly, the low status of women in conservative countries can be seen as correlating to socio-cultural factors, which contrasts with the opposite situation that exists in more liberal countries. The second view holds that all socio-cultural contexts, if the dominating and negative emphasis on male superiority were eliminated, could develop as environments that enhance the status of women and boost their empowerment in society. Action currently occurring in the liberal states of the region bears witness to this second view.

It is in this regard that the discussion on women, culture and power-sharing becomes complex and controversial. This complexity stems from the fact that, on one hand, we do not know enough about the culture of power itself, nor how this aspect is related to women. On the other, this prevailing culture and its values can be interpreted differently by different people according to certain inherent biases. This is true for at least two categories of people, those described as male or as female 'chauvinists'. While the former strive to impose male stereotypes and values on the cultural context, the latter strive to impose female values. The outcome in both instances is imbalance, thus supporting the argument for equity.

Women in Arab Power Structures

How women are viewed in Arab power structures varies from one system to another. In a fair number of countries, women have reached the very top echelons possible in the political and decision-making structures. At the moment, there are female ministers, parliamentarians and high-level administrators in many Arab states – for example, in Egypt, the Syrian Arab Republic, Morocco, Lebanon and the Libyan Arab Jamahiriya. However, elsewhere in the region, women are a long way behind. Fortunately, this situation seems to be changing, as seen in the recent decision taken by the states of Kuwait and Qatar to give women the vote.

The Prevailing Culture of Power

In my view, the lack of women's empowerment is not because they are unable to take part in power-structures, but because of the prevailing culture of power, which is dominated by males and their inherent values and stereotypes. The very idea of power-sharing is refused. Thus the existing power culture, with all the obstacles it presents to women's participation in decision-making, must somehow be changed to achieve true gender balance and equality.

It is in this context that a major shift must occur from the values and modalities of dominance to those of dialogue and partnership. This shift cannot come about through one single modality, such as legislative reforms or public awareness, but through long-range strategies on multiple tracks. These include equal access to education and knowledge, parity and participation in all forms of government and citizenship, encouragement of women's creativity and freedom of expression, equal involvement in communication and the media, and so forth.

Educating girls and women is, as the former Director-General of UNESCO states, 'the best long range investment' (Mayor, 1998). However, other measures and modalities are also important and could be extremely influential.

Power, Decision-making and Social Roles

In the Arab region, considerable progress has been achieved in some countries regarding the redistribution of social roles between men and women. Nevertheless, it is true to say that classical models remain dominant. The scope of social roles assigned to Arab women has definitely expanded from the family to other fields such as professional life, income-generating activities and participation (though limited) in political affairs. However, these new roles remain well below the level that enables women to participate effectively in social, economic and political development. The Convention on the Elimination of All Forms of Discrimination Against Women states 'that the full and complete development of a country, the welfare of the world and the cause of peace require the maximum participation of women on equal terms with men in all fields' (preambular paragraph 11). Till now, and in some societies that are dominated by male values and stereotypes, women's only role in society is that which remains within the confines of the home, running the family, raising children and doing domestic work. However, in certain countries, women have been able to break through these barriers to assume more expanded roles and functions in society.

In addition to education, *inter alia,* one significant factor in this breakthrough is the ability of women to form strong and powerful associations, grouping themselves in a more organized – even unionized – manner. In countries such as Egypt, Tunisia, Morocco, the Libyan Arab Jamahiriya, Jordan and Lebanon, women's associations have been functional for quite a long time. Their strenuous efforts, which could certainly be termed a struggle, to achieve a better status for themselves have yielded positive results, in spite of the fact that their results to date remain below expectations. This means that there remains a great deal to do in order to remove the many barriers causing the exclusion of Arab women from social decision-making.

Women and Higher Education: Issues and Perspectives, prepared for the thematic debate at the World Conference on Higher Education, identified a number of solutions for the inclusion of women, and for strengthening their roles and participation in all affairs of society. These highlight 'wider access to education, notably higher education, review of appointments and promotion procedures, provision of legislative and infrastructure support in all professions and of special programmes for women, affirmative action to favour women's access and participation while awaiting a genuine change in the attitude towards full gender equality and institutional and governmental support through clear and efficient policies which are actually enforced'.

All these measures are no doubt instrumental and effective. However, their impact is weakened if society's attitude remains negative *vis-à-vis* the social role of women and their right to share power and take part in the decision-making process.

In certain countries of the Arab region, where societal attitudes continue to discourage women's participation in social affairs, the responsibility for change has become incumbent on women themselves and on their advocacy groups.

The Islamic culture predominant in the Arab region calls for equality and encourages women to seek education, to be productive and to contribute effectively to national development. These humanistic values contradict those prevailing in societies that are the creation and product of male-dominated cultures of power. Therefore, authentic Islamic values, principles and directives should constitute points of departure for the campaigns to achieve positive attitudinal change in society so as to bring about gender balance and equality between men and women.

Another lesson could be learned from current practices in liberal Arab societies that have given women opportunities to take part in social decision-making. Numerous Arab women who were entrusted with high political and administrative positions have demonstrated great efficiency in discharging their functions. They have contributed efficiently to enriching the decision-making process, particularly in aspects relevant to women's welfare and their contribution to sustainable development. Indeed, some women have demonstrated abilities that surpassed those of men.

Based on these types of experiences, vigorous campaigns to achieve a major shift in societal attitudes must be launched in most of the Arab countries if women want to see themselves in the appropriate places in the political, social, cultural and economic structures of society. Women must take their situation in their own hands and be the primary protagonists of their own rights. They must introduce a female culture into one that is widely accepted as male-dominated and which, due to its biased values and stereotypes, is therefore flawed.

The Prevailing Concept of Feminine Leadership

No clear concept of feminine leadership in the Arab region has yet been developed or adopted. Traditionally, Arab females were not part of the power or the political structure and, therefore, very few leadership positions were attained by them. Consequently, the concept was not considered relevant.

It is only recently, perhaps during the last four decades, that some recognition has been given to the importance of broadening the social roles and responsibilities of Arab women so as to eliminate age old taboos prohibiting them from taking part in social governance. Women now selected for such positions are mainly chosen for their professional, technical and academic abilities. Also, it can be said that the advent of a critical mass of highly educated Arab females has begun to nudge them towards leadership positions. In this regard, the sheer impact of increased female enrolments in higher-education institutions in many Arab countries could be considered as a significant factor in shaping a new concept of feminine leadership in the years ahead.

Today, it is possible to find Arab women at all levels of power structures and hierarchies, although their numbers are limited. The rising numbers of female graduates are trying to break through the traditional barriers that have, for a long time, defined their social roles and limited their capacities to form new partnerships with male counterparts. Soon, we should witness a new concept of female leadership that will be compatible with the current male model. Only through this can there emerge in the future an integrated concept of leadership that is gender sensitive to the needs of both males and females. This situation will definitely lead to better integration of women in structures of power and decision-making.

Education's Role in Achieving Power-sharing

Education facilitates empowerment, which is essential for the participation of women in all aspects of the development process. Furthermore, higher education provides the expertise usually required for the key posts that shape policy in all fields. Hence, its particular importance for women is obvious.

This statement is particularly valid for Arab women and, again, the importance of the critical mass factor cannot be emphasized too strongly. No real sustained presence of women in power can come about otherwise.

Education and power-sharing are no doubt positively correlated. Clear evidence from the Arab region indicates that as the rate of women's access to higher education improves, more females are emerging as candidates for appointment to high-ranking positions in governments. This trend can neither be ignored nor reversed.

In countries where women have long enjoyed wider access to higher education, power-sharing has evolved to their benefit. In Egypt, the Syrian Arab Republic, Lebanon, Jordan and Iraq, to give only a few examples, educated women have assumed high executive and legislative positions. In other countries where this same phenomenon is more recent, positive change can also be cited, even if this is happening more slowly. However, achieving balance and equity in any society is difficult. In the Arab context, where the majority of educated persons are men, success is even more elusive. It is therefore important to strive for the creation of a gender-inclusive culture through the empowerment offered by education.

Available statistics on female enrolments in Arab systems of higher education indicate that, while their percentage in 1980 was only 31 per cent of the total number of students enrolled, this percentage had increased to 41 per cent by 1995 (UNESCO, 1998). In some Arab countries, such as Libya, the United Arab Emirates, Qatar and Kuwait, the number of females registered in higher-education institutions exceeded the number of male students.

Employment is a field where special vigilance is needed. The increased access to higher education will definitely lead to a noticeably stronger presence of female graduates in all professional fields. As a result, there will be a greater number of qualified females capable of positively contributing to development, including their participation in the decision-making process.

In a previous study, the author stated that 'apparently there is no problem preventing Arab females from enrolling in higher education; the problem comes in using the graduates, in the most appropriate ways – in work and all social affairs of the nation'. This cannot be achieved unless concrete measures are taken to eliminate social and cultural obstacles facing women in their search for employment in their fields of study (Bubtana, 1997).

If these measures are not taken, the Arab region will continue to experience existing attrition in female employment. The *Human Development Report 1998*, issued by the United Nations Development Programme (UNDP), indicated that the participation of Arab women in technical and professional jobs is still low: in Egypt, 30 per cent; Jordan, 29 per cent; Bahrain, 26 per cent; and Sudan, 29 per cent. In contrast, in some industrialized countries it reaches 50 per cent (UNDP, 1998). On the one hand, these low percentages can be attributed to the attrition phenomenon, and on the other, they can be considered a reason for limited female participation in development and power-sharing.

The author, in other studies and based on his analysis of previous trends and developments relevant to the status of Arab women in society, has expressed a certain level of optimism, saying that the 'nature of evolution will constitute the real force which will necessitate future positive changes in all areas and activities relevant to the status of Arab women and their future role in society' (Bubtana, 1999). In the same paper, the author stipulates that 'to achieve gender balance and equity in all human activities, Arab States are required to re-think and re-orient their policies and legislation which affect the roles and functions of men and women in society'. He further added that 'all reforms must be based on international conventions, declarations and instruments', the most important of which are: the Universal Declaration of Human Rights, the Convention Against Discrimination in Education and the Convention on the Elimination of All Forms of Discrimination against Women.

All these international instruments emphasize the right of women to education and employment. They seek to prevent all forms of discrimination based on sex, and deplore all forms of stereotyping (cultural, social and economic) based on male values and imposed on a good number of societies (Bubtana, 1999). What increases optimism for the future status of women in this region is that most Arab nations have ratified all these declarations and conventions. Countries are at different stages of their major reforms and changes, some are advanced, others are just starting out. As a result, the implementation of these instruments varies greatly. Women themselves must be more organized in order to stimulate the need to change and to gear this to serve their cause. Here again, the advocacy role played by women's unions and associations is crucial.

Harmonizing Cultures for Power-sharing

The two factors relevant to this subject as it pertains to the Arab region are: (1) the prevailing culture of power, which is totally male dominated and (2) the still nonexistent concept of feminine leadership – which, because this is as yet unknown and undefined, no criteria or standards exist to promote or evaluate it.

It is not impossible to harmonize or reorient traditions. However, this can be very difficult when dealing with those that are imposed by the biases of certain groups or social subsystems, and which do not necessarily stem from authentic cultural values. For the Arab region, a certain harmonization can be achieved through eliminating misconceptions as to the status and roles of Arab females. As men are largely responsible for these, through the imposition of their own values, they must necessarily be involved in efforts to change this situation.

Islam, which is the predominant cultural base in the majority of the Arab countries, gives great importance to the role of women in developing and shaping society as a whole. Throughout Islamic history, there have been quite a few Muslim females who ruled countries, became prime ministers and assumed high-level positions in governments. Very recently, three of the biggest Islamic countries elected women to the post of Prime Minister, notably Pakistan, Turkey and Bangladesh. This evidence totally refutes the claims (mainly from men) that Islam and its traditions do not permit females to participate in public life in general, nor in political life in particular (*Arab Women*, 1965, p. 10).

By pointing to these examples, it seems clear that the cultural base does not in any way stop Arab women from actively participating in these spheres. Of itself, this constitutes an important point of departure for the harmonization process. However, to yield positive results, this process must be based on a multiple-track strategy that targets all facets of the issue in question. The key components of this approach are: (1) the use of education to affirm a gender-inclusive culture; (2) the design and implementation of gender-inclusive development programmes; (3) recognition of the role of the media in sensitizing people to problems and in promoting better power-sharing and partnerships between men and women; (4) advocacy by women's organizations to reinforce their role in the whole process of reorientation and harmonization; and (5) recourse to influencing legislative structures in order to bring about positive changes, particularly those relevant to equity in employment and salaries.

Conclusions

These remarks have attempted to highlight the status of Arab women in contemporary society. Examples given in various parts of this chapter would indicate that all forms of discrimination presently practised against women stem mainly from male stereotypes, values and traditions that have been imposed by men on their local cultures. This situation has created a male-dominated context that seeks to block female participation in social and political affairs through overt obstacles and other taboos. Therefore, women's exclusion is not actually caused by cultural values and traditions *per se*, but rather by the interpretations of these imposed by their male adherents. This process has shaped socio-cultural contexts in the Arab world for so long that these are now perceived as being irrevocably male-dominated. One outcome is that the development of concepts relevant to power-sharing, feminine leadership, the new social roles of women and their place in decision-making structures have not been facilitated.

Despite this situation, a major shift has taken place in recent times, privileging the power of education and the potential of women's advocacy groups, and sweeping away old misconceptions in societal attitudes so as to nurture the emergence of a gender-inclusive culture. There is good reason to believe that a harmonizing culture – e.g., one which accepts power-sharing – is being fostered in the region. At the same time, governments are supporting initiatives to increase female enrolment at all levels of education and to promote normative action to complement this goal of equal opportunity.

The final factor of change will be the attitude of Arab women themselves with regard to their futures, coupled with their will to sustain the process under way. Women hold the key to managing the pace and nature of change in their societies – slow or steady, profound or superficial. In the final analysis, they are the masters of their own destinies.

Bibliography

Al-Amin Publishing House. 1965. *Arab Women and Democratic Transition*. Seminar convened by Ibn Khaldoun Center. Cairo.
Bubtana, A. 1997. *Women and Graduate Employment*. Paris, UNESCO.
———.1999. *The Status of Arab Women in Higher Education*. Doha, UNESCO.

Mayor, F. 1998. Preface. In: *Gender Equality Information Kit.* Paris, UNESCO.

UNDP. 1998. *Human Development Report 1998.* New York, UNDP.

UNESCO. 1998. *World Statistical Outlook on Higher Education: 1980-1995.* Paris, UNESCO.

————. 1998. 'Women and Higher Education: Issues and Perspectives'. Thematic Debate, UNESCO World Conference on Higher Education. Paris, UNESCO, p. 7.

Chapter 6

EMPOWERMENT OR POWER-SHARING? CONSIDERATIONS BASED ON GENDER-EQUITY RESEARCH IN BRAZIL

Maria Inácia D'Ávila Neto and **Cíntia Simões Pires**

In 1998, in Rio de Janeiro, we carried out field research[1] in the poorer areas of the city. The purpose was to improve people's awareness with regard to a particular community project run by the government in the Guanabara Bay area of the city.

The work among community leaders revealed a factor that cannot be considered very surprising in Brazil nowadays: 58 per cent of the 1,453 people identified as leaders were women. As one may observe in recent statistics, the tendency for women to occupy positions of leadership in Brazil is undoubtedly increasing. But, despite the positive prospects, we are still very far from being able to talk about 'power-sharing' between men and women in this country.

It is important to examine briefly the historical and cultural foundations of Brazilian society in order to have a broader understanding of this project. In colonial Brazil, there was 'an intricate complex of relations based on authority and domination involving the seigneurial world. This consisted of the agrarian family unit and then its urban counterpart later on, those who were free – coloured or white – but poor, and the social macrocosm, represented by the religious, administrative and judicial institutions that ruled the colonial life' (Fernandes, 1976). We could label the variations in existing power as: 'domestic power', 'seigneurial power' and 'aristocratic power'. In

---

1. 'Project of Social Mobilization – Community Participation', which was part of the Programme of Pollution Management of The Guanabara Bay, executed by the Government of Rio de Janeiro State and financed by the Inter-American Development Bank (IDB).

this seigneurial and colonial world, we find the origins of our own patriarchal system, which has led to what we could define as *models* of domination or submission between men and women.

The father's authority over boys and girls was indisputable. The patriarch, the supreme master, was not used to sharing his 'supreme authority', which had only begun to be threatened by the clergy and, afterwards, by family doctors. The woman considered obedience towards her husband as a continuation of this behaviour towards her father. Furthermore, men treated black and white female slaves differently. This was especially true among the seigneurial strata. The black woman was destined to provide exclusive services (including sexual favours) to her master. At the same time, our country's Catholic tradition has fostered the emergence of 'madonnism'. This is an exaltation of the virginal woman, and is reflected in the devotion to the Virgin Mary, with whom the Brazilian people have always had great religious identification.

In fact, our patriarchal system was contradictory. On one hand, it imposed the authority of the white seigneur, master of his wife, descendants and slaves; concurrently, it glorified the woman through idealistic cults, including those related to the worship of the Virgin. Some authors have called this 'the virginity complex' (Willens, 1953). Yet another model was associated with this cult – one which attributed a *mythical* or *magical* power to coloured people, and especially to their females, who are known as *mulatas*.[2] This *mythical* power, once glorified only by authors interested in Brazilian patriarchal traits, continues to be prominent today in the cultural tourism industry.

It is significant to observe that the traditional rural patriarchy has not been supplanted by the modern urban lifestyle. Even today, these coexist, so that Brazilians – whether they live in the country or in cites – embrace both the archaic and the new in their lifestyles.

Without being simplistic, we could conclude that, in our country, psycho-sociological patterns of domination (or the male-female hierarchy) result from this duality: the patricentric aspects are evident in the authority and political power foreordained to men; the matricentric aspects, revealed as the mythical or magic power, are imputed to women. The latter, however, belong to the imaginary sphere (D'Ávila Neto, 1980).

Therefore, before thinking of empowerment or power-sharing between men and women, we have to consider the issues arising from our historic and sociological past. These force us to rethink the dynamics of tradition and innovation, as well as our passage from rural to urban life. This latter process is frequently not synchronous in character.

---

2. Portuguese word to define a woman of mixed white and black parentage.

Many Brazilian women would certainly agree with the African feminists[3] who criticize the assumptions of western feminism. This places women's claims all over the world inside the same matrix. Even though we agree that no economic or social structure has ever given visibility to the vast array of domestic tasks performed around the home, we cannot agree that the functions associated with this work – those of spouse, mother and housewife – are desired equally by women in different societies.

There is no doubt that men's domination over women has always existed in the majority of cultures. In a country such as ours, with almost continental dimensions, this reality has become contradictory.[4] Thus, any analysis of this question is bound to recognize the right to difference, while still supporting the overall objective of equality for women.

The female labour force has increased over the past decades. In Brazil, women now constitute 35 per cent of the total economically active population, meaning some 25 million people at the beginning of the 1990s. Higher education is available to only 11 per cent (or 1.7 million) of Brazil's entire population. From this total, 52 per cent are women. It is important to note that 90 per cent of teaching in primary schools is conducted by women, while in higher education, they account for only 30 per cent of the teaching personnel (Faculdade Latinoamericana de Ciencias Sociais, 1993).

In 1934, the Constitution gave women the right to vote. However, their participation in government is still only 5.2 per cent in the House of Representatives and just 2.5 per cent in the Senate.[5]

Even when they are in similar professions and functions to men, women are always paid less. This inequality continues amongst women themselves – white, black and coloured women have different levels of access to higher education and different salary scales. In particular, black and coloured women are found in large numbers in the informal job sector, and very often in domestic work.[6]

These statistics show the complexity of the situation, which reflects, in our opinion, the intricate *power net* inherited from our patriarchal system. They also illustrate that, with regard to the male-female hierarchy, the shift

3. Aminata Traore, an African feminist and sociologist, said: '*Since the body is the main concern for Western feminists, when they look at Africa they are always concerned over mutilation, polygamy, and multiple maternity. The body's integrity goes far beyond these issues. No feminist ask what we really want: if we said we want more children, it would be a catastrophe...*' Quoted by D'Ávila Neto, M.I. 1995 *Women, Culture and Development.* In D'Ávila Neto, M.I. (Org.) *Social development, challenges and strategies.* UNESCO Chair on Sustainable Development, published by UNESCO/UFRJ/FINEP, p. 235.
4. Brazil has 8.5 million km^2 and a population of 157.3 million inhabitants (1996). *Brasil em números* [Brazil in figures]. Instituto Brasileiro de Geografia e Estatística (IBGE). Rio de Janeiro, 1998. Vol. 6.
5. Seager, J. 1997. *The State of Women in the World Atlas.* London, Penguin Books.
6. Existing statistics are deficient, especially those coming from official offices.

from tradition to innovation is a process that is not intrinsically chronological in character.

Even with the increasing number of families headed by women, reaching 20 per cent at present, men continue to be regarded as the traditional head of the family. As the 'breadwinner', the man is responsible for supporting the household. This could perhaps explain why men get the best salaries and opportunities in the job market (Faculdade Latinoamericana, 1993). This still occurs even though there are more women enrolling in higher education than men. The situation obliges us to reconsider the linear approach of some development projects as proposed by international organizations. In countries such as Brazil, where the socio-cultural processes are not strictly chronological, it is difficult to establish regular causal relations between higher education and the advancement of women (D'Ávila Neto, 1996).

The current thinking of the major international financing agencies accords great importance to the empowerment of women. This theory links gender studies to the issues of sustainable development and advocates local self-reliance, free from political, economic and social resources, as a means of alleviating poverty.[7]

According to Singh and Titi (1995), the groups that need empowering include: (1) the poor; (2) those in process of impoverishment; (3) communities living in fragile socio-ecological conditions; (4) jobless, landless, and homeless people; (5) and displaced victims of war, famine and droughts. As we all know, women and children form the majority of these groups. Thus, the concept of women's empowerment has undeniable relevance.

This concept, now widely known, only came to the centre of the development debate in the 1990s (Karl, 1995). The intent is to strive for the empowerment of women, which is possible only through self-empowerment. In other words, women's strategic needs would be reached through the defense of their practical needs 'bottom-up', as defined by themselves.

It is important to emphasize that the word *empowerment* is a neologism that has not yet been incorporated to the Portuguese language. In official documents resulting from the conferences sponsored by international organizations (Agenda 21, resulting from the United Nations Conference on Environment and Development, Rio de Janeiro, 1992, and the Beijing Platform of Action, adopted at the Fourth World Conference on Women, Beijing, 1995), it appears in the Brazilian translations as 'recognition of rights', 'advancement', 'incentive to participation' and 'extension of the traditional role'. Translating 'empowerment' by all these forms, despite their correct-

7. Agenda 21 recognizes the alleviation of poverty as an important factor to attain sustainable development, mentioning empowerment in Chapter 3. Later, we read the indispensability of including women in this policy (see Chapter 3, paras. 3.7, and 3.9) as one of many mechanisms helping to fight poverty and leading to better life conditions of the population as a whole.

ness, completely obscures all the relevant theoretical construct behind the term itself. This conceals the major finality of this concept for the discourse on women's equality (Pires, 1999).

The introduction of the concept of 'power-sharing', which is suggested as an associated idea, seems to us to be a way of attenuating empowerment. No doubt it is important to share power, but, at this moment, we have not reached any satisfactory level of power with which to share. This progress should be possible through empowerment and not power-sharing, and to speak of 'sharing' seems therefore equivocal. The very vision of women's empowerment presupposes the 'bottom-up' fulfilment of practical needs, while sharing would be, as the expression indicates, a 'top-down' concession – that is to say, from men (the power-holders) to women (the powerless). Therefore, when the male-female hierarchy is in question, it seems unacceptable to consider the terms of 'empowerment' and 'power-sharing' as synonyms. We could, at the most, conceive 'power-sharing' as a stage following on from 'empowerment'.

Women's empowerment implies dimensions of socio-economic, political, technological, cultural and spiritual self-empowerment. That is why matters of education, mobilization, organization, and participation in politics and in public life are crucial, as Kelkar points out when referring to Indian women:

> The vast majority of women lack training for the articulation of their problems, which in turn prevents them from participating effectively in leadership and political decision-making. There are ideological constraints as opposed to constitutional constraints that reinforce the traditional norm that men should govern the world outside the household and women should follow their leadership (Kelkar, 1986, p.330).

We see NGOs, neighbours' associations and churches as institutions of great importance in the development of women's empowerment, due to the fact that they end up working as channels of access for their increasing social participation and awareness of rights. The very act of participation in these institutions by women portrays a movement of retreat from the privacy of the home, as well as an increase in the control of their own destinies.

Our recent experience in Rio seems to indicate that the growing number of women who play a leading role in community associations points to real empowerment in progress. There is also an increasing awareness among women about participation in decision-making processes.

Leadership training carried out with local personalities enabled them to participate in decision-making relative to the management of their own communities – in the instance of our research project, this was environmental.

This experience led us to the following considerations and proposals: women's empowerment, regardless their social class, has to consider, necessarily, the gender dimension – that is, it has to ponder the aspects of the male-female hierarchy present in their cultural traditions (D'Ávila Neto, Pires).

As defined above, women's empowerment has to go from 'inside-out' and from the 'bottom-up', in a process enabling the development of an 'emancipative awareness' (Freire, Mies, Stromquist); the training groups to empower women should contemplate four complementary aspects: cognitive, psychological, economical, and political (Stromquist, 1995).

These premises form the basis of the training and research group now working with our female community leaders, who come from a poor socioeconomic group.[8] This research follows the participatory method supported by feminist and visual-anthropology theories, and uses video techniques applied to the psycho-sociological research. These techniques are particularly relevant to the comprehension of the universe experienced by illiterate or semi-illiterate women, where the written registers are substituted by images (D'Ávila Neto, 1994). This training is conceived, both conceptually and technically, according to the participatory model, and presupposes that the gender dimension is not part of the traditional curriculum in formal education. Awareness of this dimension, associated with a close examination of local traditions, is intended to be the broadest possible. In order to be truly emancipative, this research has to cross different disciplines of formal education, as well as to walk the paths of informal education.

In Brazil's case, the patriarchal system created 'models' giving women 'powers' that are basically imaginary. This can be observed in the socio-cultural context, as it is essential to re-configure any project for women's empowerment in its political terms. This means that empowerment in psychological terms (i.e., enabling self-confidence and autonomy) must be faced as a means of access to a wider form of empowerment, leading to a deeper awareness of their rights. In this sense, it is ongoing and not definitive. Whenever empowerment assumes an emancipative character, becoming a process allowing the woman who should be empowered to understand the contradictions of the domination and submission processes, it can be said that we are really moving towards the broader objective of equality between men and women.

Women's awareness of their rights is articulated, necessarily, by the assumption that they do not have a fate that is predetermined by the biological and psycho-social characteristics attributed to them. Men and women are equally destined to enjoy the free adventure of their spirits and the creative liberty of their actions.

8. Project 'Maria, Maria'. EICOS Programme/UNESCO Chair on Sustainable Development and Gender Issues.

Bibliography

D'Ávila Neto, M.I. 1980. *O autoritarismo e a mulher: o jogo da dominação macho-fêmea no Brasil* [Authoritanariansm and woman: the game of male-female domination in Brazil]. Second edn 1994. Rio de Janeiro, Artes and Contos.

————. 1994. 'Representações sociais do corpo na sociedade brasileira contemporânea [Social representations of the body in Brazilian contemporary society]', Rio de Janeiro, *Revista de Psicologia e Práticas Sociais*, Vol. 1.

————. 1996 'Women and Development: Perspectives and Challenges within the University Curriculum'. In: Kearney, M.-L. (ed.). *Women and the University Curriculum: Gender Issues.* Paris, UNESCO; London, Jessica Kingsley, pp. 69-90.

Faculdade Latinoamericana de Ciencias Sociais. 1993. *Mulheres latino-americanas em dados.* Santiago do Chile.

Fernandes, F. 1976. 'A Sociedade Escravista do Brasil' [The slavish society of Brazil]. Paper presented in the Academy of Sciences, New York.

Karl, M. 1995. *Women and Empowerment: Participation and Decision-Making.* London, Zed. Women and World Development Series. UNESCO.

Kelkar, G. 1986. 'Indian and Chinese Experience of Women's Participation in Development'. In: Trí, H.C. *Participate in Development.* Suffolk, UNESCO, pp.323–41.

Pires, C. 1999. 'Empoderamento: Um conceito para a mulher brasileira [Empowerment: A concept for the Brazilian woman]'. Dissertation presented to the research group of Programme EICOS/UNESCO Chair, Rio de Janeiro. p. 45.

Singh, N.; Titi, V. (eds.), 1995. *Empowerment: Towards Sustainable Development.* Halifax, Fernwood Publishing.

Stromquist, N. 1995. 'La búsqueda del empoderamiento: em qué puede contribuir el campo de la educación'. In: León, Magdalena (1997). *Poder e empoderamiento de las mujeres.* Santafé de Bogotá, Tercer Mundo y UN Facultad de Ciencias Humanas, pp.75-95.

Willens, E. 1953. 'The Structure of the Brazilian Family'. *Social Forces*, Vol. 31, No. 4, p. 341.

Chapter 7

EMPOWERING AFRICAN WOMEN THROUGH HIGHER EDUCATION

Peter Katjavivi

Introduction

In Africa today, relatively low numbers of women gain access to higher education. For example, in sub-Saharan Africa, only 33 per cent of women, compared to men, enrol in higher education. This proportion is heavily clustered in the areas of medical care and teaching professions. They are very underrepresented in the fields of science and technology.

During the past two decades, there has been a large increase in enrolments at both secondary and tertiary levels. In general, this increase favours males rather than females, and the universal gender bias in institutions of higher learning still persists. Women are concentrated in education, science and health-related fields of study. However, over the years, the improvement in access to higher education for women has not been paralleled by increased participation in policy- and decision-making in institutions of higher learning. As an example, in the political arena, women represent only 10 per cent of the world's parliamentarians.

Effective strategies should be devised to facilitate more enrolments for women in higher education. The socio-cultural values that act as barriers for women to pursue higher education should be addressed and corrective measures taken. Women should be encouraged to compete for higher-level positions of decision-making. In particular, women should be given

Note: This chapter is an adaptation of the paper delivered by the author at the World Conference on Higher Education, Paris 1998.

opportunities to accede to leadership posts in higher education and in other fields where their expertise can serve development needs.

The 1993 UNESCO/Commonwealth Secretariat study, *Women in Higher Education Management*, identified key barriers preventing the participation of women in the decision-making arena. Limited access to higher education, the stress of dual family and professional roles, family attitudes and cultural stereotyping were among the identified barriers. Having women role models in key academic institutions will sensitize the learning institution on how best to develop the education system and the curricula so as to encourage more women to pursue the fields of natural science. As we move to the twenty-first century, what can we do to enhance the position of women in the academic and the technological arena? Must we pursue different strategies depending on the prevailing social and economic situation of our countries?

This short chapter focuses on the status of enrolment of women in higher learning, fields of specialization, and general constraints in access to and scope of higher education in developing countries. Based on this exposé, it then develops different scenarios on what must be done to mainstream women into the academic and technological arena of the twenty-first century. The 1997 UNESCO Statistical Yearbook is the primary source of data used in this analysis. It is supplemented with data from Namibia in order to provide an in-depth analysis of the constraints and also on what to expect regarding gender disparity in access to education in a newly independent state.

Gender Disparity in Higher Learning

Data in Table 7.1 suggest that between 1980 and 1995, access to higher education improved substantially, and that the relative changes for women outweigh those for men. As a proportion of the school-age population, there were more children enrolled in secondary and tertiary education in 1995 than there were in 1980, with much of the increase in tertiary enrolment. The gender gap in enrolment is also narrowing, particularly at the tertiary level, with women having surpassed the levels for men in the developed countries. Compared to the developed countries, ratios for the developing countries are substantially lower, but these countries have made the most gains, and the pace for women exceeds that of men. Assuming that the trend in bridging the gender gap in access to higher learning will persist into the twenty-first century, chances are that by increasing investment in higher education, women will catch up with men. The problem then is whether an increase in access to higher education will restrict women to pursuing fields of study that are compatible with their maternal roles, thus making them less competitive than men in pursuing careers in academics and technological fields. The most

Table 7.1. *Trends in secondary and tertiary gross-enrolment ratios by country group and gender*

Countries	1980		1995		Relative change (per cent)	
	Secondary	*Tertiary*	*Secondary*	*Tertiary*	*Secondary*	*Tertiary*
World total:						
Males	51.6	13.4	62.5	16.8	21.1	25.4
Females	41.1	11.1	53.4	15.6	29.9	40.5
Developed:			..			
Males	88.6	36.2	97.8	47.6	10.4	31.5
Females	89.5	36.2	100.1	54.7	11.8	51.1
Developing:						
Males	42.0	6.7	54.2	10.4	29.0	55.2
Females	28.4	3.7	43.9	7.4	54.6	100.0
Sub-Saharan Africa:						
Males	21.6	2.5	26.9	4.6	24.5	84.0
Females	12.4	0.7	21.6	2.5	74.2	257.1

(Source: 1997 UNESCO *Statistical Yearbook)*

recent data on graduates at the third level of education by fields of study (1997 UNESCO *Statistical Yearbook*) support this phenomenon.

Data for the United States, the United Kingdom and Germany, the primary host countries for students from other countries (in particular, from developing countries), and South Africa, which plays the same role in sub-Saharan Africa, shown in the charts overleaf, illustrate the universal gender bias in enrolment in institutions of higher learning. Women are concentrated in education science and health-related fields, while engineering – the main technological field – is the men's domain. Thus, to be effective, actions targeted at enhancing career opportunities for women in the technological fields must include incentives that would minimize the stress in fulfilling their dual roles within family and career.

Constraints to Higher Learning in Developing Countries

Investment in higher education is a function of the level of social, economic and cultural development (UNESCO, 1997). Further, because of scarce financial and human resources, developing countries rationalize their investments in institutions of higher learning by targeting activities that meet the basic requirements of the country and are also economically most profitable. As a result, only study programmes that maximize social, economic and cultural returns are offered within these countries. To compensate for the

Chart 7.1. *USA: graduates at the third level of education by field of study and gender in 1995*

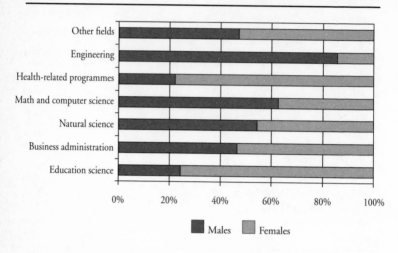

Chart 7.2. *South Africa: graduates at the third level of education by field of study and gender in 1994*

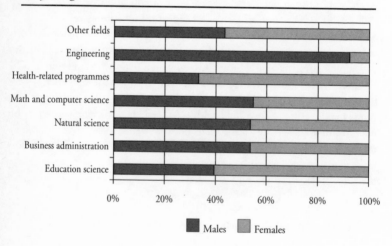

Chart 7.3. *Germany: graduates at the third level of education by field of study and gender in 1994*

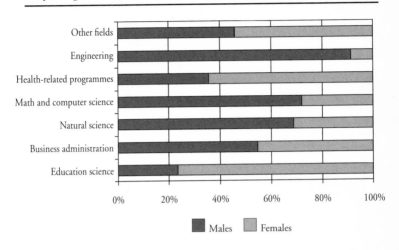

Chart 7.4. *United Kingdom: graduates at the third level of education by field of study and gender in 1995*

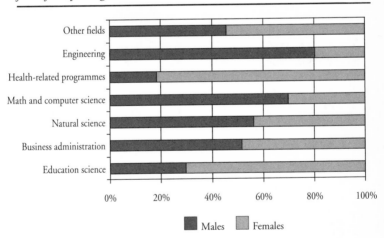

demand of qualified people in highly specialized professional fields, students are sponsored to study in other countries. This arrangement conflicts with the desire of some women to be mothers while pursuing their professional ambitions. It is easier for women to surmount the challenges of family care and professional ambitions in their own countries, as they can always rely on the extended family support system, if the need arises.

Social, cultural and economic factors make studying outside their countries more convenient for men than for women. The social structure in the developing countries pressure women into getting married and starting a family ahead of professional considerations. Our culture also expects women to bear the burden of caring for the young, the elderly and the sick. The overall welfare of the family also falls on women, forcing them to supplement the family's income. The more educated they are, the more they can provide for their families, particularly if they are employed in the male-dominated professions. However, once they are married, women redefine their professional aspirations in the context of their cultural obligations. If the learning or working environment has support facilities that minimize women's burden of care-giving, more of them will pursue postgraduate studies, including the engineering and other technological fields.

Women and Higher Learning in Namibia

In Namibia, women's involvement in the struggle for independence afforded them a unique role in the country's policy decision-making process. In 1995, out of thirty-six cabinet and sub-cabinet positions, women occupied six, while in the national assembly there is one woman for every five men (University of Namibia, 1997). As shown in Table 7.2, women are underrepresented in the leadership positions at the University of Namibia, possibly because they lack the desired academic qualifications.

At the time of Namibia's independence in 1990, the few well-educated Namibians had studied in other countries. As already indicated, chances were that only a small number of women had such an opportunity. In subsequent years, following independence, more Namibian students have enrolled at the University of Namibia. Since its establishment, the university has also developed some postgraduate study programmes in a few of the faculties. The scope of the fields of study or postgraduate studies has not matured to the level of producing fully fledged academicians, let alone those who could qualify for the top positions. Thus, women are underrepresented at the most senior positions at the University of Namibia, partly because they lack the desired academic qualifications. Table 7.3 on student enrolment at the university supports this.

As shown, women are concentrated in the fields of medical and health sciences, education and humanities and social sciences. There are also rela-

Table 7.2. *Gender composition of University of Namibia employees in 1997*

Academic staff	Male	Female	Total
Professor	19	2	21
Associate professor	19	3	22
Senior lecturer/Librarian/Researcher	32	17	49
Lecturer/Librarian/Researcher	55	57	112
Other	21	38	59
Total	146	117	263

Non-academic staff	Male	Female	Total
Top management	7	0	7
Senior management and high-level specialists	14	1	15
Middle-level management and other specialists	36	40	76
Other	99	108	207
Total	156	149	305

Source: University of Namibia, 1997.

Table 7.3. *Student enrolment by faculty and sex for various years*

Faculty	Number of Students					
	1992		1994		1996	
	Males	Females	Males	Females	Males	Females
Agriculture & Natural Resources	*	*	*	*	20	8
Economics & Management Science	117	91	217	146	313	253
Education	154	204	237	234	370	405
Humanities & Social Sciences	137	147	178	218	196	213
Law	*	*	12	11	41	25
Medical & Health Science	62	573	112	645	94	534
Science	73	32	103	46	161	80
Centre for External Studies	227	373	242	479	253	549

* No enrolments – New Faculty.
Source: University of Namibia, 1997

tively large numbers of female students for whom it is possible to pursue studies through distance learning. However, these occur in fewer numbers in the science and technologically-related fields. Thus, to be effective in bringing women into the fields of science and technology, incentives or motivations aimed at enhancing career opportunities for women in these fields must be developed.

In attempting to promote the participation of women in higher education, it is necessary to develop an understanding of the situation at the secondary and primary school end of the education spectrum. Figure 7.1 summarizes the enrolment pattern by sex in Namibia's primary and secondary schools.

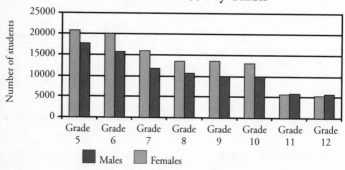

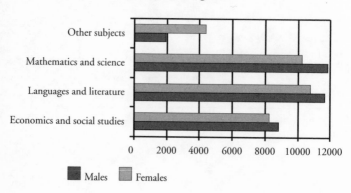

Fig. 7.1. *Primary- and secondary-school enrolments in Namibia by sex for selected years*

Given the enrolments shown in the charts above, one would have expected that, other things being equal, female and male student representation at the university would be the same in all the fields. But this is not what happens. The Faculties of Medical and Health Science (producing nurses) and Education (producing teachers) take most of the female students at the university – as can be seen in Figure 7.2.

Full-time female students at the University of Namibia in 1991–95 by field of study

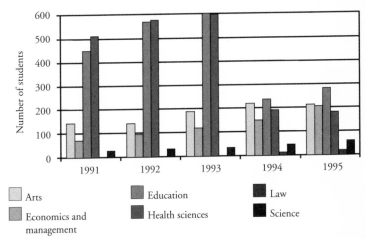

Full-time male students at the University of Namibia in 1991–95 by field of study

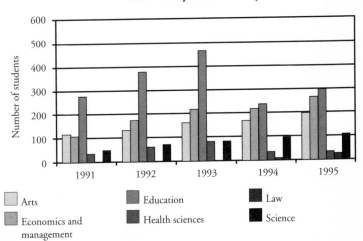

Fig. 7.2. *Full-time enrolment at the University of Namibia for females and males, by field of study, 1991–95*

In addition to gender equalization in the fields of study at the University of Namibia, the previous charts imply that the country has had to make choices on which fields of study to offer at the University of Namibia. Because of resource constraints, the university offers very few fields of study. For instance, law was offered starting from the 1994 student intake, and engineering is not even offered yet. In 1994, there were a total of 1,626 full-time students enrolled at the University of Namibia (CSO, 1997), while 1,747 Namibian students were enrolled at institutions of higher learning in South Africa (UNESCO, 1997. *Statistical Yearbook*). This implies that, at university level, there are more students enrolled outside than within Namibia. Even though data are not available by sex, it can be speculated that the numbers are not the same for females and males, and that more of the latter are likely.

It should further be noted that the University of Namibia is not only faced with the issues of staff equity in terms of gender, but also with capacity-building. While this is one of main priority areas in the development of the university, can we ensure that women are given equal opportunity in this process? Are they readily available to compete with their male counterparts? Do they possess the desired requirements? Who makes the decisions for recruitment and absorption to the academic community? All these are issues that will need to be looked into.

Strategies for Mainstreaming Women in Higher Learning

It is worth emphasizing that education facilitates empowerment, one of the essential tools in decision-making. At the present time there are far too few women at the higher levels of decision-making, partly because they do not possess the necessary educational qualifications. Higher education provides the expertise usually required for key posts that shape policy in all areas. The importance of higher education for women is therefore crucial. In a study by UNESCO/Commonwealth Secretariat (1993), three key factors were considered as necessary to enable women to accede to leadership posts in higher education. These are: (1) societal attitudes to women, which discourage their participation in decision-making; (2) their lower enrolments in higher education; and (3) the absence of a gender dimension in the higher-education curriculum.

With regard to decision-making, the same study noted that the principal barriers preventing female participation were, among others: (1) limited access to education, especially higher education; (2) discriminatory promotion practices; (3) the stresses of dual family and professional roles; (4) career interruptions; (5) propagation of the glass-ceiling syndrome that privileges covert criteria for advancement; and (6) absence of adequate policies and legislation to ensure the participation of women.

With regard to *the way forward*, the four recommendations made are: (1) to provide women with a solid foundation in mathematics and science subjects; (2) to discourage the system of tracking students into arts and science streams at the second level of education, as practised in some countries; (3) to provide childcare facilities at the institution of higher learning or, in situations where particular fields of study have to be pursued in another country, create special funding for married women so that their spouses can accompany them; and (4) to provide a means through which the issues of gender inequality can be addressed both formally and informally, at all levels of society.

In Namibia we are addressing some of these issues. We have a Gender Training and Research Project at the university, funded by the Government of the Netherlands, with the main objective of promoting gender awareness in the university community and incorporating gender studies in the curricula. Namibia is one of the countries in East, Central and Southern Africa that have been involved in a SIDA-funded regional project on the production and promotion of gender statistics. The Government of Namibia has created the Department of Women's Affairs, under the Office of the President, with the specific objective of promoting gender awareness and addressing issues relating to gender inequity in the country.

Conclusion

As a final thought, it may seem that this chapter has pointed to problems rather than to their solutions. Many of the areas that must be remedied have their roots in the ancient cultural traditions of Africa, where women had clearly defined but separate domains of influence. These will obviously be very difficult to accommodate as the region seeks to position itself in relation to global trends affecting all sectors, including higher education. Yet we must not be deterred in meeting this need to harmonize the old habits and new priorities. Let me refer to the Declaration and Action Plan on Higher Education in Africa, adopted at the African Regional Consultation (Dakar, April 1997) in preparation for the 1998 World Conference on Higher Education. This accorded special recognition to the role and responsibilities of women in African development. There was a strong call for policies to remove gender inequity in education and to promote the advancement of women in African society. Strategies cited were affirmative action, the mobilization of women's advocacy groups and greater emphasis on the relevance of gender research as a source of data to shape policy. Moreover, a commitment was sought to double the number of women – as students, teachers and decision-makers – in higher education in the region during the coming decade. These are worthy objectives for higher education in Africa, but their attainment will depend on a major shift in cultural attitudes. This would seem to be the most complex challenge facing the region today.

Bibliography

Central Statistical Office (NPC), 1996. Statistical Abstract, Namibia.

UNESCO, 1995. *Policy Paper for Change and Development in Higher Education,* Paris.

———. 1997. *Statistical Yearbook.*

———. 1998. *Higher Education and Women: Issues and Perspectives. World Conference on Higher Education,* Paris.

UNESCO/Commonwealth Secretariat, 1993. *Women in Higher Education Management.*

University of Namibia, 1997. *Beyond Inequalities: Women in Namibia.*

University of Namibia, 1995-1999. *First Five Year Development Plan.*

University of Namibia, 1996. *Annual Report.*

Chapter 8

Empowering Women in the Community: The University's Role

Judith Mbula Bahemuka and Susan Van der Vynckt

Introduction

In November 1995, the UNESCO Special Project for Women, Higher Education and Development was launched as a six-year initiative of the UNITWIN/UNESCO Chairs Programme. This project is designed to strengthen the role of women in higher education and their participation in training and research. It supports UNITWIN/UNESCO inter-university networks on training in management for women academics and administrators in co-operation with the Association of Commonwealth Universities and the Inter-American Organization for Higher Education. In selected universities, the Special Project supports UNESCO Chairs that focus on new orientations to research and training in a number of key areas, including science and technology, sustainable development, culture and development, gender, basic education and health.

The UNESCO Special Project has an important contribution to make at a time when UNESCO and others are increasingly concerned with the need for higher-education institutions to provide intellectual and research support to inform the development process. Universities are often dubbed 'ivory towers', despite their indisputable task to produce relevant research and training, and to engage in the generation, dissemination and banking of knowledge. However, the degree to which universities – especially those in developing countries – can participate in development research is hampered by a number of factors. University staff and students lack time to participate in action-orientated research. Academic programmes have become so crowded that neither students nor lecturers have the time to engage in any meaningful research activities. Universities are often underfunded, and thin budgets limit research opportunities. The tendency is toward theoretical rather than practical applied work. Finally, university staff are reluctant to mobilize action given that this is not a prime consideration in their recruitment into university service.

UNESCO Chair on Women, Basic Education, Health and Sustainable Development

In 1996, UNESCO and the University of Nairobi started cooperating on the establishment of a UNESCO Chair on Women, Basic Education, Health and Sustainable Development. The idea was to establish a UNESCO Chair with a programme of work that could contribute to the achievement of basic education for all in Kenya through community-based research and actions that enhance the quality and conditions of learning while addressing the needs of girls and women. More specifically, the work plan aims to: (1) strengthen the capacity of the university to contribute to the formulation of effective policies and programmes for basic education; (2) develop an interdisciplinary and participatory approach for the identification of constraints, needs, expectations and aspirations for education of learners, parents and other members of the community; (3) sensitize and mobilize communities in support of education through the development of tangible and innovative interventions aimed to improve educational access and participation; (4) identify stakeholders in education at all levels including teachers, educational authorities, teachers' unions, civic bodies, etc., and to enhance their capacity through partnership-building and networking; (5) advocate for policy formulation and implementation; and (6) undertake participatory monitoring and evaluation of actions, and measure the impact of activities in terms of results and sustainability.

In the planning of the University of Nairobi UNESCO Chair, serious effort was made to mobilize faculty members, along with undergraduate and graduate students, to become closely involved in the operational research, analysis and integration. The Chair itself was appropriately placed in the Department of Sociology,[1] whose prime mandate is interdisciplinary, thus covering key aspects relevant to women, basic education and primary health-care. Other departments of the University of Nairobi have been involved in the training and research (e.g., nutrition, community health, health economics, development studies and education).

---

1. Professor Judith Mbula Bahemuka is the designated UNESCO Chair holder.

Focus on Basic Education and Gender Inequalities

The UNESCO Chair on Women, Basic Education, Health and Sustainable Development has pioneered training and research capacity-building in basic education while maintaining a strong focus on gender issues. From the onset, there has been a strong awareness that the university (like others in the country) has been lacking in intellectual support and research critical to the development of basic education that meets the needs at school and community levels, especially for girls and women. The intent has been to find ways to overcome obstacles to educational participation along gender, socio-economic, cultural and other lines, while at the same time emphasizing responsiveness to local concerns, constraints, expectations and needs. The guiding principle has been that the university must play a more active role through training and research in the development of basic education and the formation of educational policies connected with 'education for all' objectives, especially as these relate to the promotion and improvement of female education.

It was recognized that the central issues in basic education in Kenya and other countries of the Africa region remain access and equity. Equitable participation in basic education, particularly primary education, is an important goal of social policy in all countries, because access to this level is the foundation of the education system and the basis for subsequent selections to other levels and to lifetime opportunities. Other important issues related to basic education – especially to primary education – touch on the questions of educational quality, efficiency and relevance. The UNESCO Chair has been addressing a number of areas, such as the need for a better understanding of the magnitude of significant educational deprivations still existant at different levels, for example, between rural and urban areas, across regions, among different groups and social classes and along gender lines. Here, gender is considered an important basis of inequality, because it crosses all other categorisations such as age, ethnicity, regional social class and area of residence.

Development Concerns and Relevance

The work of the UNESCO Chair is timely in light of findings of the poverty-assessment study conducted by the World Bank in 1996 in Kenya, which revealed no improvement during the decade 1982-92 in the proportion of the rural population below the poverty line – around 50 per cent. Moreover, the proportion of urban poor in 1992 below the poverty line is around 30 per cent. The report indicates that children from poor families have less schooling, are more likely to be malnourished, are less likely to be immunized and face higher chances of dying during childhood. The lack of sustained, per capita income growth, along with unequal distribution of education and health-care benefits, are identified as factors contributing to the increase in the numbers of poor in the country.

There is a significant gender imbalance against women which reflects a complex combination of historical, socio-economic, socio-cultural, and past and present policy factors. This has resulted in unequal educational opportunities for boys and girls, starting at the age at which they are enrolled in school. Gender inequalities persist through the first and second levels of education, with more girls dropping out of school than boys. Particularly high attrition rates are noted among female students from disadvantaged social origins. This in turn determines their accessibility to higher-education opportunities and, eventually, to the location of women on the occupational ladder.

There are a number of factors associated with the lack of concern and investment in the education of girls in Kenya and many other countries. The fewer girls than boys found in all levels of the education system is in part due to the culturally perceived priority in importance of the education of boys over that of girls. Families facing economic hardships are often forced to make difficult decisions about the schooling of their children, but in general, such decision-making tends to favour the education of boys. It may be that financial returns for girls' education are considerably smaller than those of boys, as girls will eventually marry and leave their parents. There is also the prevalent belief, especially among men, that educated women cannot be controlled as easily (by them), and that education opens opportunities for women to obtain material independence from men.

Some of the key questions that have shaped our research agenda are:

1. How do families or households living in conditions of poverty determine who goes to school?
2. How do they determine who is withdrawn from school?
3. Who in the family, or household, makes decisions about the children's education?
4. Are different decision-making processes operative with regard to access to and withdrawal from school when female offspring are involved?
5. What are the critical points at which decisions are made – regarding who goes to school, who stays in school and who is withdrawn from school?

The UNESCO Chair has been seeking answers to these fundamental questions, and searching for a better understanding of the family's – or household's – decision-making processes that these imply, and considering how the insights derived can be applied to the formulation of policies and programmes to promote female empowerment through education.

While examining factors that constrain girls' education at the family and household level, we have also recognized the need to understand more about the educational establishments themselves and the specific learning environments these provide. Another concern has been to understand how communities support their schools, and why they may have become disengaged from them. It is not surprising that learning environments are often not compatible with expectations for optimal performance of learners and educators. Many schools, especially in rural areas, are poorly equipped and staffed, and lack basic amenities.

Linking education to better health and well-being

Women with schooling tend to marry later and delay childbearing, are more likely to practise family planning, healthy living behaviours and safe hygiene, and to see to it that their children are properly fed and receive treatment promptly when ill. Despite the close association between female education, family health and child survival, the number of illiterate women continues to increase (in absolute terms). In this connection, the UNESCO Chair has investigated undernutrition and ill-health as important underlying factors of low school enrolment, absenteeism, poor scholastic performance and early school dropout among both girls and boys, especially in disadvantaged groups and regions. Recent findings on child health, nutrition and educational participation affirm the widespread prevalence of undernutrition, common communicable infections, and diseases among the school population.

Much childhood undernutrition and ill-health could be prevented through reaching underserved groups – especially girls and women – with: (1) basic education that includes health education; (2) through improving living conditions (notably in relation to water and sanitation); and (3) through enhancing the social and economic context of people's lives. In policy terms, addressing the health and nutritional problems of the school-age population is not only important for the general well-being of this group, but also fundamental in the struggle to democratise access to and participation in basic education for both girls and boys.

With a better understanding of the health and nutritional situation, we have been exploring ways and means to make education and the curriculum more relevant to the needs of all learners, especially girls. We have been focusing attention on the life-skills area, given the prevalence of poor nutrition, schoolgirl pregnancies, forced child marriages, female circumcision, violence and sexual abuse. Education on the prevention of HIV/AIDS has become a high priority as infection rates have increased among the young. Our challenge here is to effectively promote education for HIV/AIDS prevention that is sensitive and responsive to the complex socio-cultural, ethnic and economic aspects of young people's lives.

From Analysis to Action

There are many social and cultural hurdles for girls and women to over-come. Many of these are due to gender biases and the underrepresentation of girls and women in educational institutions at all levels. Empowering women in this society and others must include equality of opportunities in education. Educational institutions will need to improve the delivery and quality of their services to better meet the needs of girls and women. Empowerment through education will involve more and more women in development matters – from the household to the community, and through to national levels. The research and training being carried out through the UNESCO Chair on Women, Basic Education, Health and Sustainable Development at the University of Nairobi should contribute to the process of policy and programme formation, with the purpose of fostering both a gender-inclusive culture and empowerment through education to promote healthy and sustainable development.

Bibliography

World Bank. 1996. *Assessing Poverty in Kenya. Africa Region*, No. 55.

Part III

WOMEN, POWER AND THE ACADEMY

Chapter 9

CULTURE AND FEMININE LEADERSHIP

Sheryl Bond

Introduction

The fundamental changes that are occurring worldwide in the areas of democratization, globalization, regionalization, polarization, marginalization and technology are transforming societies. This transformation, while important and necessary, is often painfully difficult for individuals and for the institutions that provide the social and political frameworks for interpersonal and international relationships.

For society to move with deliberation through the course of events, while sustaining or providing a reasonable quality of life for its citizenry, is a formidable challenge requiring all the talent, experience and expertise available in society. If it is not to cripple its own efforts in order to persevere, it is vital that society effectively utilize the talent, experience and expertise of women in all levels of decision-making.

The principle and practice of full and equal partnership of women and men is in itself a significant reform in gender roles, and is yet to be achieved. To the extent that this partnership is underdeveloped, so, too, is the ability of society to address the other critical areas of reform. Education in general, and universities in particular, have a special formative and exemplary role to play in fully engaging talented women in all aspects of academic life.

Note: This chapter is based on research on feminine leadership carried out by the author for UNESCO and the Inter-American Organization for Higher Education.

Cultural Contexts

As social institutions, universities exist within cultural and historical contexts that exert tremendous influence in the shaping of the university's culture, the structure of academic work and the definition and/or expectation of institutional leadership. While considered as one of society's most enduring institutions, the university has survived, in part, because it has been able to adapt at the local level. Local contexts powerfully shape the life of a university. In addition to its adaptability to the larger social context, the character of an individual institution can vary over time. The deeply embedded assumptions and values inherent in an institution are derived from its institutional history, size, age and reputation; whether it is public or private, religious or secular; or if it enjoys the full- or part-time commitment of its students and faculty. It is the culture of the institution that dictates the ways in which a particular university may respond to changing contexts and expectations.

A pattern of variability in the participation rate of women in higher education, by country or region, is also manifest in the percentage of women holding faculty appointments. At the level of institutional leadership in a senior administrative capacity, the numbers of women participating in the life of the university are significantly low across all regions.

The subject of culture in relation to trust and power-sharing has become particularly salient. From findings of a number of meetings and workshops on this topic, a clear consensus has now emerged that culture, as it was and had been understood for a significant period of time, was the single most important factor in creating an environment in which women were undermined and/or blocked from assuming the highest levels of leadership. General consensus has been reached on the impact of cultural values. In particular, culture is the most significant variable in that it: .

1. held women and men within socially prescribed roles that undermine the health and the quality of life of a country;
2. ascribes to the contributions of men a greater significance than it ascribes to those of women;
3. extracts a much higher personal cost from women who seek and/or accept leadership positions than it does from men; and
4. assigns a particular, often implicit, norm to the behaviours expected of a leader. Also, this norm is so exclusive and demands such a high personal price – from men as well as women – that it drives out alternative patterns of leadership.

The impact of culture on the potential power-sharing is significant. In particular, it generates a situation that nurtures a lack of trust. Many men do not trust a woman to be loyal, to understand what men expect of her, or to act as a man would be expected to act when in a position of power and responsibility. The tendency to mistrust women is equal to the vulnerability felt by the men whose own lives and careers rise and fall with women's. No leader can effectively work to improve the quality of life of her people without the trust of men as well as of women. The importance of trust, and how it is generated and maintained among diverse peoples, is a critical issue that is yet to be discussed openly and honestly. This discussion must now begin to take place.

Leadership in the Academy

Leadership can and does occur in all domains of academic activity. Teachers define who will be taught, what will be taught, how it will be taught and the standards of evaluating what has been learned. Leaders in teaching are imbued with an extraordinary ability to know critical teaching points, excite students and peers about learning, and know what teaching practices are most effective; they invest their considerable energies into the promotion of student learning, as well as modelling a new kind of leadership concerning planning, methodology, use of pedagogical resources and assessment in an increasingly teacher-student oriented partnership.

Researchers define questions and seek answers. Leaders in research have the ability to identify and answer particularly important questions and to seek connectivity, and are also driven to communicate their work to others.

Leadership exercised by persons of significant influence is a force that guides and can shape the institution. Individuals holding senior administrative offices are vested with the responsibility – whether derived by statute, charter or articles of incorporation – for ensuring that the institution and its members fulfil their educational, social and ethical mandates. In a university, leadership responsibilities reside both in the position and with the individual who holds the office at any time. Persons in leadership posts may or may not be leaders in either teaching or research, but may be respected for their judgement, credibility, institutional knowledge and predictive powers. Such individuals are usually drawn into the institutional structure through appointment to senior administrative posts.

While holding a leadership post does not in itself guarantee a person is a leader, the person speaks to the academy – including its students, staff and external constituencies – about what the academy is and what it is doing or could be doing better, and provides a contextual framework with which to guide the institution's progress towards its goals. In so doing, a senior administrator, through the use of influence, shapes the standards and, through the judicious use of authority, monitors the application of those standards to the appointment of those admitted to professorial posts as well as those identified as leaders.

Beyond the Numbers Issue

Those holding leadership posts in higher-education institutions have a uniquely important function in shaping the institution, which will play such a crucial role in shaping knowledge and the future. It is, therefore, particularly critical that there be an equal partnership of women and men at the most senior levels within the academy to ensure that women exercise their right and responsibility to serve the university through the provision of their own intellectual and moral leadership.

The inclusion of the talent, beliefs and life experiences of women as well as of men is changing the academy in fundamental ways. The discovery of knowledge is an activity of individual inspiration, initiative and enlightenment, even if it takes place in the context of the institution or the codification of a discipline, and with peers engaged in like activities. The influences that lead to discovery are not merely scholarly, but include personality, life experiences and cultural contexts. Bringing about a partnership of women and men in the academy is bringing about a change in the nature of the institution.

To the extent that there is a continuing absence or underrepresentation of women at the senior levels of the university, the 'deficit' is the responsibility of the institution itself. The deficit cannot be addressed unless one knows what factors impinge on the choices made by senior administrators – and particularly by women senior administrators – as perceived by the individuals concerned.

The 'G.O.E.S.' Paradigm[1]

The continuing underutilization of the talent and expertise of women within the university is a significant detriment to the quality and the adaptability of the institution to the society that it serves. The continuing dearth of women in senior administrative positions in organizations in general has been the subject of investigation, discussion and, frequently, divisive debate. In this regard, two theoretical perspectives have dominated.

The first perspective is a *person-centred* view, in which the paucity of women is attributed to the psycho-social attributes, including personality characteristics, attitudes and behavioural skills of women themselves. The 'problem' is vested in the individual, and she is called upon to adapt herself to the traditional male concept of management within the academy.

An alternate theoretical perspective has emerged to explain the data. The *structure-centred* paradigm advances the view that it is the disadvantageous

2 G = gender; O = positional power; E = environment; S = system.

position of women in the organization structures (few numbers, little power, limited access to resources and marginalization of role) that shapes and defines the behaviour of women. The underlying premise of this perspective is that men and women are equally capable and committed to assuming positions of leadership. The 'problem' is vested in the structure, and the remedy is a fundamental change to eliminate inappropriate discrimination in institutional policies and practices.

Despite the initial optimism of their respective creators, neither perspective has been able to explain the continuing lack of significant progress for women. In addition, the tendency toward 'exclusivity' inherent in each paradigm may well have generated more divisiveness than dialogue as answers and remedies continue to be sought. Neither paradigm has made provision for the possibility of an interactive effect among the variables in the two models. Such limitations in the assumptions and the methodology of gathering and analysing data appear to have led to an overly simplistic interpretation of findings in studies of gender and leadership.

An understanding of the reasons for the continuing underrepresentation of women is far more complex than has been thought. A comprehensive programme of action research has, over the last five years, examined this question from the personal perspective of women and men currently holding administrative posts in universities in Asia and the Americas. Data gathered from these parallel studies have alerted us to the strong possibility that both the power level and the social context might be important factors in understanding how decision-making, within a strong academic ethos, differs between women and men.

In the attempt to address the methodological problems identified in earlier studies, we can create a new paradigm in which both simple comparisons and multivariate analyses of variance could be made to account for the effect of 'G', *gender* (sex/role attributes), 'O', *positional power* (level of appointment, access to resources, value of the person's knowledge and expertise to the institution), 'E', *environment* (institutional and cultural context) and 'S', *system* (interaction between 'G', 'O' and 'E'). This analysis highlights the importance of individual power level and institutional size as important variables that help to explain existing assumptions and stereotypes. However, it also specifically confirms or refutes a substantial number of pre-existing perceptions in these domains.

Stimuli and Barriers to Feminine Leadership

In 1997, a survey of Latin American women holding executive posts in universities of the region produced a checklist of factors that can either promote or impede their access to such positions:

- *The need to interact with peers*
- *The marginalization of talent*
- *Politics before merit*
- *Posts of confidence*
- *Many paths to leadership*
- *The 'Superwoman' syndrome*
- *Lives built on self-respect and service*
- *Leaving my father's house (i.e., family conflict caused by a woman's decision to pursue a career)*
- *Ability to be crafters of their own careers*
- *The complexity of women's lives, requiring a huge capacity for work*
- *A belief in the university that sustains commitment*
- *The fact that women possess and use a wide range of personal attributes as leaders*
- *The numbers of institutions that recognize talented women*
- *Recognition of merit*
- *Uneven progress toward an equal partnership, and the importance of exemplary institutions in this regard.*

It is widely acknowledged that these elements probably exist in all regional contexts – and hence across all cultures. Further research is warranted to understand the specific culture-based aspects of these phenomena that have gained a certain degree of commonality.

Moving Towards Partnership

A variety of strategies can make significant differences to the numbers of women appointed to and successfully fulfilling the leadership responsibilities inherent in senior administrative posts, as described below.

1. *The diverse lives of women.* Women leaders come from and represent diverse backgrounds, styles and areas of expertise. Depending on the institutional context, cultural context and power level, as well as type of post (academic or professional) held, the career experiences of women may also differ. Management strategies must reflect and respect this diversity.
2. *Leaders are educators who can change the university as well as basic education.* Education has been and continues to be the vehicle by which women have changed their lives and the lives of others. The origins of values that emphasize the importance of education, the necessity for economic independence and the commitment to service come, for some women in the study, primarily from within the family. Others

were more likely to learn these values from teachers, travel or other social experiences and political processes.

3. *The continuing absence of facts.* There is a continuing absence of reliable data about the status of women in universities, including their advancement to senior decision-making posts, salary levels and other terms of appointment, and advancement beyond the institution to senior posts in government.

4. *The importance of developing networks.* To build on the knowledge and expertise of women leaders currently in senior posts, and to encourage other women to seek senior leadership appointments, formal networks of leaders in higher education within the different regions need to be established.

5. *Career paths and personal lives.* The advancement of women extends beyond equal access to creating an environment in which the impact of senior leadership on the lives of women can be accommodated without undue stress.

6. *Women today as pioneers.* The women holding senior leadership posts today are usually the first women to hold their posts, and thus can mentor others succeeding them. Ways in which positive mentoring can be recognized as a feature of holding senior posts require more investigation and support.

7. *The impact of 'champions' on institutional change.* The lack – or underrepresentation – of women at the most senior levels of influence within the university is a problem for the institution, and it requires the participation of women and men, through dialogue and action, to be addressed adequately. Up until now, with very few if any women holding the most significant positions of administrative leadership, most 'champions' have been men. Yet, while talking with these 'champions', it was not unusual to find that their efforts were dedicated to the memories of their mothers, who themselves were prohibited by cultural norms and historical circumstances from realizing their dreams and potential.

8. *Recognition of merit.* Both women and men holding leadership positions told us how much they would appreciate more recognition for their work. However, much more needs to be done, both through private and public effort, to recognize meritorious work of women leaders.

9. *The advancement of women and the advancement of the institution.* In the future, initiatives to promote the full participation of women in all aspects of academic life and that focus on this critical relationship will, undoubtedly, be more effective than those that do not.

Chapter 10

MAKING UNIVERSITIES GENDER-AWARE: THE SWEDISH EXPERIENCE

Berit Olsson and **Christina Ullenius**

Introduction

The World Conference on Higher Education was an exciting event. Never before did so many people gather to look at the future of higher education and research. Never before did governments, university leaders, non-governmental organizations (NGOs) and other interest groups meet in such numbers at this level to examine the issue before us: how can we make universities gender-aware?

UNESCO is to be congratulated on the initiative to bring gender issues to the forefront of the discussion and to underline the responsibility of member states and their governments, as well as institutions of higher learning and research, to correct existing imbalances.

We would like to pay tribute to all of those who have worked and fought in order to bring attention to gender inequities. The issue has far too long been a task for NGOs and activists alone. Today, it is on the agenda of institutions and governments, who are now prepared to take action. The problem now is *how*. However, we must learn from each other – when it comes to women in academic positions, we in Scandinavia are not more advanced than many countries in Africa, Asia and Latin America. Our university leaders have a lot to learn from others.

The Swedish Experience

This chapter reports on some aspects of recent Swedish experiences. During the past four years, some bold and decisive steps were taken by the recent Minister of Education, Carl Tham.

Sweden has long been regarded as one of the most advanced countries concerning equality between men and women. Yet, four years ago, 93 per cent of the professors in Swedish colleges and universities were men, despite the fact that women have been admitted to higher education for 120 years, and despite the fact that more than 60 per cent of Swedish university students were women. This deficiency within the academic world was considered completely unacceptable.

Equality within higher education and scientific research is not just a question of justice, but also a question of democracy and of academic quality. The participation of women and men, and the inclusion of gender perspectives in curricula, as well as in research, makes it possible to cover a broader field of knowledge, involve students to a greater extent, provide young women with role models and give women a visibility in the academic world, as well as in society in general.

Today, there are no formal obstacles preventing women from reaching high positions in colleges and universities. Nevertheless, men dominate all levels of influence. This situation is not just a remnant of the past. On closer examination, it becomes apparent that progress towards gender equality is a very slow process. There were even indications that the process was beginning to stagnate in several educational areas. Now, however, the rhetoric has changed. Few would challenge the need for more women in higher education and research. Nevertheless, discrimination against women continues.

It should be pointed out that in Sweden, the major drop-out rate of women occurs at the postgraduate level. We are fully aware that, in many other countries, decisive action must be taken at all levels - from primary and secondary education to higher education and research.

Government Actions Taken

The Swedish government decided on a package of decisive actions for higher education and research, and allocated resources for their implementation. Among these were extensive allocations for new positions from the postgraduate to the professorial level in order to correct the underrepresentation of women. A number of new academic positions for women have been established: thirty-two full professors, ten guest chairs, seventy-three assistant professors and forty post-doctoral positions.

Targets have also been established for the further recruitment of women professors. In ten years' time, at least 25 per cent of all professors should be women. Setting goals for the highest level of the university hierarchy is expected to have a favourable effect for women at all levels within the academic community.

Instructions have been issued for educational and scientific institutions to shoulder the responsibility for addressing gender imbalances, and several measures have been taken to organize and promote gender studies.

This action package was met with antagonism in some quarters, and with great support in others. It gave rise to a debate that focused on objectivity in the academic world. It became evident that, contrary to the general assumption, the academic world was far from objective, and unintentionally, discriminated against women.

Table 10.1. *Summary of actions taken by the Swedish Parliament or Government from 1996–2000*

New positions for the underrepresented sex in various scientific fields
    32 chairs (professorships) (compare with circa 1,500 existing Chairs)
    10 Chairs for female guest professors
    73 research assistants (first level of academic career)
    40 post-doctoral positions
    120 positions for doctoral students
    Financial resources to support the programme

Resources for gender research
    6 academic fields have been identified as fields of particular interest to receive financial support for:
        – one professor
        – one research assistant
        – one doctoral student

Secretariat for gender research
    To support gender research in various fields and in various institutions in Sweden.
    To be responsible for new interdisciplinary research group at the Linköping University.
    Instructions to the Swedish Research Councils to promote equality between sexes, and to include and promote gender perspectives in research being supported by these bodies.

(Source: Presentation of B. Olsson and C. Williams at the World Conference on Higher Education)

Female Appointments

Two Swedish researchers, Christine Wennerås and Agnes Wold, looked at how men and women were judged when applying for research positions. The findings, published in *Nature* in 1997 under the title 'Nepotism and Sexism in Peer Review', were initially challenged, but later scrutinized and found to be valid. They demonstrated some of the mechanisms behind the exclusion of women from leading positions and research funding.

Wennerås and Wold showed that, in the peer evaluation of the applicant's competence, all other factors being equal, men were rated higher. Another factor that came through was whether or not the applicant was known to the appointment committee. These two 'qualifications' turned out to have surprisingly decisive consequences. In practice, the double disability of being a woman and lacking personal contacts appeared, but only with difficulty, to be compensated by scientific achievements.

Even if this study is unique, its findings are certainly not unique to the Swedish Medical Research Council and other organizations in Sweden or other countries. Within the academic community, there is a tendency to play down the subjective element, to speak of research as fundamentally objective. Indeed, this study has put this assumption into question.

Scientific and academic competence are concepts that have evolved in what has been a male-dominated world. Nevertheless, they are considered to be gender-neutral. The consequence is that today, gender is a basis for segregation in colleges and universities. Students encounter a male-dominated world from the very beginning. Most of the teachers and administrators are men; most of the chosen literature is written by men; and studies often concern the problems of men and research by men.

Mainstreaming and Special Actions

This is why gender issues have to be seen as a field of knowledge, both as an area of study in its own right and, equally important, as an integral element in curricula in all relevant subjects of education. This is part of what is often called 'mainstreaming'.

Mainstreaming alone, however, is not enough. In Sweden, such efforts have been supported by other means as well. A series of courses has been directed to vice-chancellors and other high-level staff to improve their knowledge and awareness. These courses have not primarily focused on attitudes, but on facts and figures demonstrating how men and women are affected by measures believed to be gender-neutral.

Research

Special attention has been given to the organization and promotion of gender studies as a field of knowledge. Gender research has an important task in exposing the social mechanisms of culture, customs and tradition that create the female and male characteristics in society. It may disclose mechanisms that continue to prevent women from improving their situation, despite legislation and economic opportunities. This is true as well within the academic world itself.

Gender research is necessary to answer questions of why women and men remain traditional in their professional and educational choices. In the physical sciences and engineering, women account for only about one-fifth of graduates. Within teaching and health-care programmes, the situation is reversed. These fields are largely dominated by women.

To create a society in which all people are given the opportunity to develop themselves on the basis of their ability and interests, we need research that analyses the importance of gender, as well as of class and ethnicity. Democracy as well benefits from the perspectives provided by different groups.

Impact

It is far too early to assess the impact of these actions. However, there are many promising signs. The number of women in high-level positions has increased, and they have been positively received. Universities have started special recruitment efforts, and annually report on their progress. Many students have reacted to the lack of women teachers and researchers, and they have begun to ask how this can affect their studies, their interest in their subject and their choice of a future career. To an increasing degree, the students have begun to demand a discussion into the fact that the literature in almost all courses is overwhelmingly written by men, and that gender is never used as a starting point for analyses. In addition, the Scientific Councils have started to demand that a gender-based perspective is considered in research proposals. How are men and women affected by societal change, technological development or other phenomenon under study? Thus, gender studies have now been accepted as an important field of knowledge. Several universities have Chairs for gender-oriented subjects, e.g., Political Science with a gender perspective. Finally, special Chairs in Gender Science have been established in some of the new universities, e.g., in Karlstad, as well as in Lund, one of the prestigious older ones.

In short, something has started to change. Most people recognize that equality between women and men affects the quality both of the academic institutions and of society at large. We believe that the achievement of equality between men and women does not happen all by itself. Action has to be taken by the government, by the institutions of higher education, by NGOs and by individuals. Finally, much can be achieved on the international level. International co-operation among universities, staff and students can help us look at ourselves with a new perspective, and we can learn a lot from each other.

The role of UNESCO, however, goes far beyond promoting and facilitating co-operation. By its analytical function and normative role, UNESCO has a major role in advocacy on all levels, and its lead in these important efforts is welcomed by the international higher-education community.

Chapter 11

WOMEN IN UNIVERSITY POWER STRUCTURES

Robyn Munford and Sylvia Rumball

This chapter is based on our experience of working in universities, which has included involvement in senior management, teaching and research. It is the outcome of a series of conversations between us as we attempted to make sense of what we were observing and experiencing, and to support each other in what are essentially lonely positions.

Women in University Senior-management Structures

Until now the gender debate in universities has tended to focus on issues of student access and participation, with particular emphasis on enhancing the presence of women in science, technology and engineering. Overall, the percentage of women students enrolled in universities is improving, albeit with imbalances still persisting in some countries and in particular areas.

There has, however, been less emphasis on the participation of women in university at senior-management levels, and hence a disappointing lack of progress, despite increasing attention to human rights and equal-employment-opportunity (EEO) programmes at government and institutional levels. Currently, only 7 per cent of universities worldwide are led by women. In New Zealand, while no universities are led by women (although women have been short-listed for recent vice-chancellor appointments), women now hold positions as heads of department/school/institute, deans, and assistant vice-chancellors/deputy vice-chancellors/pro vice-chancellors. Our own experiences are derived from serving as a dean of faculty and a head of school. In these roles we have had to be both the leader of a unit, as well as a member of the executive branch of a larger unit. The two roles provided different experiences. In addition, our experiences as leaders of a unit were affected by the gender make-up of our respective units (predominantly male versus predominantly female) and the different academic areas (science versus social sciences).

Without doubt, the lack of women in top management posts in universities is in part a reflection of the career patterns of women in the lower academic ranks, where domestic responsibilities may make slow and difficult progress. We ourselves have walked the part-time path as we balanced work and children, and we acknowledge the career delay that resulted for ourselves. However, we too would support the argument put forward in the report on the Thematic Debate on Women and Higher Education, held at the World Conference on Higher Education (Paris, 5-9 October 1998), that this imbalance also has structural origins stemming from cultural traditions based on a view of the relationship between the sexes that emphasized the notion of male dominance and superiority. Jane Jakeman, in *The Oxford Magazine*, discussed the underpromotion of women in the academic ranks as follows:

> It may be that the collegiate university has run its course, that it is a survival of male bonding systems that cannot accommodate the wider world, a network of rock-pools full of stranded creatures. In any event, it is open to charges that here lie the real bastions of male dominance, for the University may commit itself to reform as much as it likes, but the maxim that entrenched power will never yield voluntarily will be borne out as long as the colleges retain autonomy. (Jakeman, 1994)

Sheryl Bond (Bond, 1997) suggests that senior positions are seen as 'posts of confidence', and it seems that many men, consciously or unconsciously, do not believe that women possess the necessary attributes to carry out important responsibilities in a fully reliable fashion. Hence, they are reluctant to share decision-making processes with women.

Ironically, at the present time, there is tremendous pressure on women to show their willingness to compete and to take on leadership roles. This puts women in a very difficult position – on the one hand, they are under pressure to apply for senior-management positions, yet aware of the consequences to their career prospects and self-esteem of being repeatedly unsuccessful and hence potentially labelled as unable to carry out leadership roles.

In addition to the effects of traditional power imbalances, women in university environments in New Zealand are currently experiencing the effects of restructuring. Policies and procedures for implementing new structures include casualization, downsizing, managerialism, competition, accountability, performance indicators and merged institutions.

One particular aspect of this environment of fewer positions and increasingly scarce resources is that as competition at all levels increases, so does competition between women. Indeed, women may be asked to collude with men against other women, and in many instances, women may be played off against one another without being aware of what is happening.

Relationship of Women to Power Structures

It has been our experience that imbalances in power are often not openly addressed. While EEO policies have attempted to challenge the situation of women in universities, these policies rarely address the roots of the imbalance, as demonstrated by a range of behaviours and attitudes exhibited by those in authority towards those of lesser rank, which includes the majority of women academics. While the behaviours are not inherently male or female, in our experience they are displayed more often by men, as men currently hold most of the management positions. Some examples are:

1. criticism and exploitation of support staff (these staff are often women);
2. aggressive communication styles and dominance of speaking time;
3. patronizing attitudes towards women;
4. sidelining of group members;
5. belittling people and/or their ideas;
6. not listening to or according value to opinions different from their own;
7. use of analogies that are unfamiliar to women;
8. the adoption of a judgemental and subjective approach that prejudges people and puts them into categories (good and bad);
9. use of in-jokes and humour to exclude those who do not buy into the dominant modes of operating;
10. taking criticism of ideas personally (this personalization of criticism has the potential for damaging impact on the person who dared to criticize);
11. making deals outside formal meetings;
12. presenting quick decision-making as a sign of strong leadership and discussion, compromise and negotiation as a sign of weak leadership; and
13. talking over, at or down to people, rather than engaging in true dialogue.

If these situations are challenged, the challenger may be accused of not playing the game and not being tough enough to cope with difficult situations. All the above strategies help to maintain the status quo and thus prevent others from sharing in power. Inevitably, power relations are difficult to disrupt as (understandably) people in power generally operate so as to maintain their own positions, while maintaining others in positions of dependency.

In our experience, academic women often do not take the time for in-depth reflection upon their relationships with power structures. Rather, they are more likely to put their heads down and get on with the task at hand in order to implement their vision for research and teaching. Moreover, it may be difficult and painful for women to acknowledge that power does exist and that they may be excluded from decision-making processes. Further, the actual process used for decision-making and the time allowed for it may take them by surprise. Women tend to consult widely and view issues from a range of perspectives and positions prior to making a decision. Many of the women we have worked alongside clearly demonstrate a willingness to explore alternative ways of decision-making. However, they are often challenged for this willingness and find themselves criticized for operating in different paradigms.

For many women it comes as a shock to discover that, despite the burgeoning literature on EEO, they will not necessarily be sought out for higher office or encouraged to be part of decision-making processes. When confronted head-on with power structures, they may feel unable to name the issue, and unable to find women with whom to share their dilemmas. If women do make it to positions of power, they may feel isolated as they realize that they are in uncomfortable positions. For example, do they challenge the exclusion of women and risk being ostracized, or do they remain silent? Both strategies have drawbacks and negative consequences.

Given the downsizing of academic environments and their increasingly competitive nature, we predict that in the future women are likely to find it more difficult to achieve senior-management positions. We also predict that women academics may be very cautious about seeking such positions.

If women do choose to apply for senior positions, they may take many risks. They may find that, while they are short-listed, their inclusion on the short list may be no more than an acknowledgement of EEO. If unsuccessful in their application, they may find that the attempt has jeopardized the success of future applications, as employers are suspicious of applicants with a record of unsuccessful applications.

Challenges to Women in University Senior Management

One of the challenges often faced is whether to take a stand on an issue. Are we courageous enough to offer an opinion? Can we function with the spotlight on us in what might feel to be an unsupportive environment? We are continually having to weigh up the pros and cons of speaking out.

We are also often asking ourselves whether those with whom we interact support open and transparent decision-making. At times we have suspected that colleagues, forced to operate in this way, have suffered a sense of loss when intrigue, mystique and lobbying were no longer a part of the decision-making process. In addition, we suspect that people in power often engage in back-room deals because they are unwilling to face conflict and take risks.

Further, we, as women who have found ourselves at times in positions of power, are now facing up to the fact that changes we have made when in those positions have not survived our departure, leaving us with the knowledge that our colleagues went along with these new approaches only because they had to, not because they believed in them. The cultural change was temporary, rather than permanent. The remaining lesson is that the prevailing culture is going to be very difficult to change.

A particular challenge we have faced is our own self-doubt. As we sit around the table as members of an executive team, we find ourselves continually reflecting on our roles, finding it difficult sometimes to convince ourselves that our presence is valued. We ask ourselves: are we fully included? Is the decision-making process a real one or are we just going through the motions, and not really being asked for an honest opinion? Has a situation been pre-judged, and the decision already made? Is our opinion going to count?

As a result of experiences of this type, we know of some women (and indeed some men) who are choosing to move out of senior-management positions rather than work for and with people who do not share their vision for how things should be done. Women can feel much discomfort and tension particularly if they work in a mode that seems contrary to their own philosophy. It requires considerable courage to acknowledge the potentially damaging effects of a lack of congruence between beliefs and behaviour, or values and actions, and decide that there may be other ways for achieving goals. This understanding means that sometimes we may opt for a sideways step as our next career move.

Building Alternative Leadership Structures

The following draws on our experiences of senior management and provides suggestions for creating a more inclusive environment based on power-sharing (Munford et al., 1999).

1. *Vision.* Be clear about one's vision, create opportunities to share this vision with others and continually reflect upon this vision. Keep asking what we are trying to achieve, and for whom. Check how our vision fits with wider structures.

2. *Analysis.* Analysis is essential for exploring power-sharing and how to transform power structures. Alternative ways of operating need to be

clearly articulated. Analysis goes hand in hand with strategies for change – both are important and necessary. Strategies without analysis can be directionless.

(3) *Building partnerships.* Strategies for building partnerships must be clearly articulated. Alliances must be forged with a wide range of groups including not just our students, but also groups outside the university environment. Partnerships may also include identifying the need for pastoral care, so that students and staff feel supported in the university environment. We must always check that our practices reflect our goals of equity and power-sharing, for example flexible work practices, so that a wider group of people are involved in the work environment.

(4) *Reflection.* Reflection is a key strategy for achieving power-sharing. This reflection should take place on a regular basis, and should be linked to our analysis and strategies for change. Our ideals must continually be juxtaposed with reality.

Education for Change – Changing the Culture

The culture in universities in New Zealand was inherited from the United Kingdom. It is based on hierarchies and élitism and, hence, by inference, exclusion. Superimposed on this inherited culture is a pioneer culture that has revered individualism, physical prowess and toughness. This, then, is our legacy, and we predict that real change, as opposed to superficial change, will take decades. Nevertheless, those of us who have achieved senior positions and who are committed to women-friendly management practices remain optimistic that we can make a difference – albeit a small one – and that our efforts are worthwhile.

So what are some of the approaches that can be used? Modelling the changes for others is effective, as values and attitudes are best taught by modelling desirable behaviours, such as inclusive decision-making processes, transparency, consistency and honesty. Structured teaching can be used to show alternative ways of operating. This can include an analysis of current situations and the posing of alternative scenarios in order to develop new environments. Research can show up contradictions, and be used to provide alternative scenarios and roles for women. Challenging custom and practice is also a key strategy. For example, speaking up about inappropriate behaviour, which has its risks in that we may have to put ourselves apart from the dominant view, and supporting equal-employment policies. Women need to assist in the implementation and monitoring of these in order to ensure that they are indeed honoured. In New Zealand, such policies are supported by legislation at a national level.

We believe that implementation of these approaches will contribute to the creation of a better environment in universities, one that staff – and female staff in particular – will find more comfortable. Over time, we hope that this change will make it easier for women to flourish in senior-management positions, which should in time lead to greater numbers of female managers.

Some Conclusions

1. Power-sharing in a senior-management position is a risk. There is the anxiety of losing the respect of female colleagues, and the tension of too much or too little buy-in from colleagues.
2. Some of the challenges we take on can threaten our personal situation as well as our physical and emotional health, and we may find that relationships with those in our home environments can be affected.
3. We need to learn from the experiences, both good and bad, of women who have already held senior-management positions in universities.
4. We must be critical and honest about whether we are being effective in our current environments, or whether we should be thinking of alternative strategies and positions.
5. If we are to engage in power-sharing and in reforming hierarchical and exclusive environments, we must put supports around ourselves. This includes supporting women who are in senior-management positions and whose management style can provide a model of best practice.
6. We must know how to celebrate our successes and how to share these with others.

Bibliography

Bond, S. 1997. *Service and Self-respect: Women Leaders in Latin American Universities.* New Papers on Higher Education – Studies and Research, No. 19, p. 11.

Jakeman, J. 1994. 'Rock pools', *The Oxford Magazine*, Issue 104, Trinity Term.

Munford, R.; Selby, R.; Walsh-Tapiata, W.; Baskerville, M. 1999. 'Pushing the Boundaries; Women's Experience of University Environments'. In: *Winds of Change: Women and the Culture of Universities International Conference*, Sydney, University of Technology. *Conference Proceedings*, pp. 236–42.

Chapter 12

GENDER, CULTURE AND POWER-SHARING IN ACADEMIA

Anne Holden Rønning

Introduction

If a gender balance in power-sharing in academia is to be achieved, then the elimination of cultural barriers, as well as entrenched cultural attitudes, is essential. In the wake of the debates at the World Conference on Higher Education in 1998, we must consider what measures should be taken. The chapters in this publication illustrate how the situation varies from continent to continent. Here, I should like to focus on some of the major issues that need addressing if change is to take place.

The socio-cultural nature of power in institutions of education is historically based from the time of the medieval seats of learning. Their task was to help and tell people how to interpret the world around them. Women were participatory in this, whether in convents or among the upper echelons of society. Much feminist research over the last two decades has brought to light the number of powerful women in learning and other walks of life prior to the nineteenth century who consistently took up a plea for equality in knowledge, power for women and the need for attitudinal change. These women wrote not just to criticize men's attitudes to and ideas about women, but also to empower women themselves. Certain authors point out here that this situation is still current in some parts of the world. The question of empowerment, as D'Ávila Neto states, is not the same as power-sharing. She

Note: Thanks to Associate Professors Sigrid Kaland, Kari Losnedahl and Lise Opdahl, University of Bergen, Norway, and to Professor Edward Ingebretsen S.J., Georgetown University, U.S., for their helpful comments.

is not alone in having problems with the translation of empowerment into Portuguese, as it is equally problematic in other languages. This highlights one of the many problems in discussions of the kind in this book. They are conducted on the power premises of an English-speaking élite who do not always account for the variability of language. Does power mean different things in different environments? Undoubtedly so, dependent on the stage that development has reached.

To return to the world of education, academics are, or should be, the intellectual leaders of a nation, and therefore concerned with the controversial arguments of the society in which they live, including its global component. Their role is not only in the academic world, but also in the real world,[1] as many of the nineteenth-century technological devices and advancements that we are reaping the benefit of today prove.[2] Academia is no longer élitist but embraces a far wider range of institutions – from high-powered research establishments to regional colleges – as well as a diversity of subject areas, fields of research and educational offers. It is 130 years since women gained access to higher education, but still they are few and far between at decision-making levels. Why should one half of the population still be underrepresented at the decision-making level of this important aspect of contemporary society?

Traditionally, feminist approaches to issues of this kind have been to point out all the ways in which it is difficult to reach the top – what is known as the 'glass-ceiling syndrome'. Surely, the time has come to move away from this negativism, and focus rather on the reasons why, although the sky is the limit and is visible through the doors and the ceiling, women still do not reach the top in many professions. To equate gender with power is misguided and, as we go into the twenty-first century, potentially problematic. Some of the chapters here have rightly queried whether we can share something that by definition is hierarchical. I would suggest that cultural barriers and attitudes in academia are not gender-based, but power-based, in a system that is still top-down, despite various attempts at democratization. In our search for change, we should perhaps not look at gender and power, but rather analyse the nature of the culture of power in organizations and propose some strategies for change.

Changing the Culture of Power

Within the framework of the theme of this book, we are usually thinking in terms of 'culture' as a closed society, often an integrated whole, where even

2. I choose to use the word 'real' rather than the conventional 'outside' world, as this implies the ivory-tower syndrome of which élitism is often accused.
3. For example, film (1895), television (1883), radio (1896) and electromagnetic waves (1887).

changes within that society will nevertheless allow it to remain closed. Part of the power structure in an organization is to ignore that gender exists as a factor of power, and that custom underscores and forms relations. This reinforces what is common for the group and makes opposition difficult. Though this implies that ideas about culture and its interpretation are static, barriers are more fluid than seems apparent given the notion of organizational culture. A culture can be changed by the introduction of new symbols, new values, ideas and aims. To bring about this change, certain factors need addressing: the culture of power, organizational change, the language of power and positive-discrimination systems.

The Culture of Power

The culture of power is still much a result and perpetuation of the patriarchal and hierarchical system, which means that those at the top, and those who pull seniority and expertise, are those who determine what others have to do and what is acceptable. Within all academic environments, the need for attitudinal change is essential if the dominant power culture is to be altered, as present systems have many negative approaches with strong elements of internal politics and power-building. However, having said this, we must beware of the danger in academia of a state of cultural amnesia, a forgetting of the purpose of higher education.

The protégé system favours the perpetuation of the old-boy network, what Irigaray has called 'the between-men cultural world' (1993, p. 21), since many male professors give priority to male students, and the lack of female professors means the imbalance is retained. The suspicion of 'those who are not one of us' creates secret hidden barriers that are insurmountable for those outside. The system of credit and promotion is often vicious, and appears at times incidental. Established and accepted views, what might be called 'group-research interests' within several departments and institutes, though positive in the sense of establishing an environment friendly to research, can also be negative for those who wish to pursue other paths of knowledge, and can also perpetuate a certain aspect of knowledge, giving it an air of sacredness, though others may characterize it as conservative. This can explain why, though the number of women in doctoral programmes is high, when it comes to tenured positions they do not have the same opportunities. In some institutions, another aspect of the culture of power is the tendency to recruit their own graduates, that is, people who will fit into the pattern devised for that institution. The culture thus becomes embedded and, though in certain fields, such as science and medicine, this can be justified as rational given the enormous cost involved in equipment, in other fields it can cause stagnation.

Another aspect of the culture of power today is the use of technology. There is increasing pressure to include information technology in every aspect of a subject. If you do not have information technology in courses, then they are out of date, yet nobody is asking whether information technology is really needed in all subjects. Increased use of technology can be in conflict with creativity, as technological expertise can well be at the cost of aesthetic quality. This field is largely male-dominated (though not because women are computer-illiterate) and thus constitutes yet another reinforcement of the male culture of power in academia that is also a disturbing one, as it is the future they are commanding. Counter-measures must be taken.

Pressure to conform to the standards and norms of one's institution are great, as research funding is often linked to those wielding power. One method is to ignore either non-traditional research that is not directly linked to the subject areas in which the academic is employed or their international activities when it comes to promotion. The culture of power within academia is thus entrenched in a meritocracy that is determined by some few. Interdisciplinarity has yet to become fully acknowledged, so many of those presently researching interdisciplinary fields are at a disadvantage, as such courses are often thought of as suspect – i.e., taken out of personal interest – and are often misunderstood, women's and gender studies being a case in point. Recognition must be given for promotion to those who venture into these fields, but this is not the case at present. Many academics are under this kind of cultural pressure – sometimes but not always gender-based; more often, a form of psychological harassment that is subtle rather than direct, and thus so much more difficult to deal with and counteract.

Capitalist and market-driven forces are increasingly putting the value of the employee in terms of cost and results, not the individual, as all that matters. This is a trend already apparent in higher education, which is disastrous for intellectual thought as it ignores the learning process and the gradual evolution of ground-breaking intellectual research. The dictates of evaluation systems demanded by politicians and linked to funding are destroying the nature of academic study, in particular some aesthetic subjects. This often results in the redirecting of funding from certain subject areas to others, and the creation of new fields of studies at the expense of established ones. There is a general failure to sit back and look at the purpose of a university and its role, which cannot be determined by short-term economic gains and market-led models, but which as an establishment must entrust a population with the skills and a fund of universal knowledge to monitor what the politicians do and what global changes will occur.

In addition, another new culture of power within academe has arisen over the last ten to fifteen years, in that, increasingly, power is being moved from the academic to the management staff. In a world where a knowledge of business-management systems is important, we should not forget that the management is there to serve the employees, in this case the academic staff. A recent article in a Norwegian paper suggested that leaders within universities should see themselves as being in the 'service' of the academic staff, not as 'suppliers' of work for academic staff. What is happening in many universities today is that management has taken over the role of running the university as a business, where the employees are not really consulted, and where an understanding of the complexities of academic research and teaching are neither understood nor always given priority.

The Linguistic Discourse of Power

The culture of power can be seen as a discursive practice. Much research has been done on gender differences in language, and language as the most important identifying feature of a person. As Irigaray says, 'Sexual difference ... conditions language and is conditioned by it' (1993, p. 20). These differences may be in pronunciation and grammar, in gender-preferential language, the linguistic culture of a specific work environment and in body language. This can be an important reason why women do not enter decision-making positions. Either they may not want to adapt to the linguistic codes of their employer, or they may be unable to communicate in those terms. The question of the difference between meaningfulness and intelligibility in language is relevant in matters such as giving compliments or different conversational practices, e.g. silences, interruptions, inadequate or delayed responses, not answering, and the use of 'I' or 'we'. As Coates asks, must women, if they want power, 'adopt the more adversarial, information-focused style characteristic of all-male talk, and typical of talk in the public domain?' (1998, p. 295). If so, do they then become unfeminine? She also asks 'Should we see gender and power as being in a both/and relationship or an either/or?' (1998, p. 375) A failure to comprehend the complexity of discoursive linguistic practices, and how language reflects, constructs and maintains male dominance, can lead to a split-and-divide mentality, for, as Neto points out in her article, how can the culture of power be gender-neutral when the language used to express it is masculine?

Organizational Change

Much research has been done on the question of organizational change, the relationship of gender and power, and how a better balance can be brought about (Gerhardi, 1995; Hzin and Newman, 1995; Ledwith and Colgan, 1996). Two possible models seem relevant in relation to getting a better gender balance in decision-making positions in academia.

One method is a so-called 'cultural approach' that is 'a performative definition of organizational culture as the system of meanings produced and reproduced when people interact' (Gerhardi, 1995, p. 20). Each workplace has its own system of meanings formed by language, thought processes and cultural symbols. Like any organizational culture, academic people share the same symbols – but the gender interpretation of these may be different. The problem in this kind of culture, as indicated above, is that for everyone who has their place in the system, power is often exercised by silencing opposition, as well as the fact that invisible mechanisms often operate.

Another model is what is known as 'new managerialist culture'. This is more long-term in contrast to the short-term competitive culture. The individual is more central, and people are supposed to be put in a position to enable them to give more. Effectiveness is not the only criterion as the individual's development is also valued, but even here the idea is that we are partners, meaning we do things together and inspire each other, without stating the source of our inspiration.

However, are either of these models applicable to academia? Though in both cases partnership and the sense of belonging to an environment are stressed, it still seems apparent that power-sharing is based on terms dictated by the group rather than by the individual. We can therefore query whether attitudinal change will really infiltrate the system. The individual may find her/himself power-sharing not as a partner on her/his premises, but on predetermined factors that are not gender-neutral.

Positive-discrimination Systems

Some of the chapters in this book have dealt with positive-discrimination systems, and see these as one solution to getting a better gender balance in decision-making positions. The Nordic countries have had such a system for many years, and although Sweden has now proposed a special system of appointing female professors, experience of such systems is not entirely positive. Comments such as 'you got your position because you are a woman' have not been uncommon, even to people who are or were not part of any quota system. Equality laws also query the legality of such measures.

Even the positive results of promoting women may have unintended negative effects. When Gro Harlem Brundtland became Prime Minister of Norway, she brought seventeen women into government, thereby establishing a convention by which no government in Norway today will form a government without sixteen or seventeen women in ministerial positions. However, despite this, there is a downside. Quota systems for women have meant that governments – not just in Norway – consider they have the female expertise in-house, and therefore do not need to approach gender-specific non-governmental organizations for input in the same manner. It is utterly false to assume that women will always give the female view, or men the male – gender research has proven this. In academia, quota systems have an additional negative effect, in that the few women at the top are over-worked so long as all committees, whether administrative or academic, have met their requirement to have one-third to 40 per cent women.

Strategies for Sharing Responsibility and Authority

Many women express a lack of interest in applying for decision-making posi-tions, given the cultural criteria listed above. They would rather do their own research when the possibility of having any real influence on change is min-imal. If a gender balance is to be attained, and men and women want to join and stay within academia, then all these aspects of the culture of power must be addressed and strategies introduced before power-sharing is possible.

The culture of mass higher education is one of consumerism, and no longer that of an élite. Those who choose not to continue their studies do so consciously, as they are not sure that higher education is in fact going to provide them with a culture and an experience that will benefit them in the long run. This also applies to brilliant graduates who, though interested in an academic career, choose to opt out, including those women who do not want to go on to decision-making positions. Certain strategies at various stages of the life cycle would help to alleviate this problem. Rumball has listed alternative leadership structures and some of the ways in which change can be brought about. In addition, I should like to add:

1. *Mentoring systems and leadership training.* The introduction of men-toring systems, where nonexistent, is a strategy that would help younger members of staff. Time-management skills could be taught and leadership training given. In-house training must be given in academia, but not when people reach the top or are elected to posi-tions of power. It should be, alongside obligatory pedagogical training (possibly even integrated into that), a prerequisite for any teaching or research job that there is an understanding of the fact that leadership is job-specific, though the skills learnt can be transferred to other fields. In academia, this entails a closer working with the outside world, which is what we are sending our students out into. It should not be only the economic colleges that provide that sort of training. The initiative has to be pedagogically based – it is not a question of co-operation for financial reasons, which is one of the inherent dan-gers, and may be why so many academics are sceptical of modern management methodology. Part of leadership training must also be to

learn to market oneself, something at which women are traditionally bad due to their socialization when young.

2. *Promotion and tenure.* A revision of the promotion system is funda-mental to recruitment and diversity among academic staff. The tenure system and doctoral programmes are not exactly gender-friendly, as this kind of qualifying process takes place at a time when young peo-ple are in the process of establishing relationships and families, so the demands on time from academia and home are enormous. Many choose therefore to opt out, especially women who tend to see other values in life than work alone. In itself, this should be no problem, but age is often a hindrance to further progression up the scale of merit, another vicious aspect of the system that affects both genders equally at an age when men also want to play their role as fathers. This is espe-cially the case in the Nordic countries. Given that this is often the time couples may seek to have children, a tenure-and-promotion sys-tem that is dependent on what one has published or written within the last five or six years is both a physical and psychological strain.

3. *Ageism.* Present systems of promotion are unfavourable to the person who enters the academic path at a later stage in life, or wants to reenter after time spent out of the work force. Age as a determinant is discrimi-natory and gender-hostile. Physically, many women in their late for-ties/early fifties have a surge of energy that could well be utilized for top positions, as international appointments have shown. They have fin-ished their family responsibilities and aquired a wealth of experience that is often undervalued. At this stage of their careers, many men are worn out, having had little opportunity to diversify. Recruitment should attach more weight to nonacademic skills, all other qualifications being equal. For example, the mature woman with a doctorate should be seen as an asset, as she brings not only academic qualifications, but also nego-tiating skills and life experience learnt in other environments. As educa-tors of the next generation, this kind of life experience can be invaluable.

4. *Environment.* Infrastructure, regarding buildings as well as equip-ment, is poor in many academic environments. Institutions, espe-cially state-funded ones, are unable to compete with the business world in terms of facilities and funding, let alone salaries. If universi-ties want to get the best brains for research and the education of the next generation, something drastic must be done about the quality of the work environment offered to academics in many fields, though of course there are exceptions. The United States has understood this far better, as is pointed out by Professor Cora Kaplan in the *Times Higher Education Supplement* (23 April 1999, 0. 15): 'the major state-funded universities as well as the big private institutions ... encourage and support teaching and research by seeing that scholars are allowed to

focus on these.' Is a top job attractive in an environment that appears not to respect the needs of its employees?

Conclusion

The multifaceted nature of leadership needs to be addressed. *Time* magazine, in a section on 'The Global Leadership Challenge', comments on the need for training in leadership. It is not something that is inherent in mankind. According to Warren Bennis of the University of South Carolina, 'The new leader is one who commits people to action, who converts followers into leaders, and who can convert leaders into agents of change' (*Time*, 24 May, 1999). Heterogeneity and diversity in any work-force create opportunities, but also present challenges. I do not think that more women in the decision-making process will necessarily effect change. Rather, the contrary: there is an inherent danger, as women politicians have shown, that having reached the top, they expect other women to make it, too. This underscores the need for attitudinal change and different ways of work.

Many men and women have acquired parental skills, such as experience in negotiating between family members, the organization of a household and different activities – a highly skilled plan in many families – and participatory skills learned in helping with children's activities. Given the right encouragement and recognition of such skills, I am of the opinion that more women would be willing to pursue long-term careers within academia and would apply for decision-making positions. The democratization of leadership that has supposedly taken place has not brought with it a softening of demands. Instead, it has raised the level of requirements. Leadership is about coping; so is parenting.

The question of a style of leadership called 'feminine leadership' has been touched on in some of these chapters. In my opinion, there is no such thing as feminine leadership, as this inherently classifies it as second rate given the gender bias against the feminine. If what is meant by 'feminine leadership' is the possession of qualities that are considered more female-related than male-related, what Lips has described as 'democratic and interpersonally oriented' (1998, p. 4), then we have only to look at some of the many women leaders of recent times and ask whether they were introducing a new kind of leadership, or simply playing the male role. This 'powerful woman' role may be underlined by media presentation, whether in the news or soap operas.

The second wave of feminism has given many women the opportunity to take on decision-making positions in politics or elsewhere. But has this brought more gender-friendly values, the 'soft' values, the human component, the ability to carry out what is known as human-resource management? Is this what we mean by feminine leadership, a more sharing- and partnership-based approach to leadership? In the Nordic countries, young women are playing the game men have traditionally played. This has evoked certain socio-cultural results, such as the men choosing the father/parent role rather than the earning one, and demanding work conditions that allow them to take family responsibility. If this trend continues, then real power-sharing can become a reality, and the question of gender in power structures will become irrelevant. We already see tendencies in this direction.

Finally, a word of warning in the battle for gender equality and power-sharing. One cultural barrier that is increasing rapidly is the feminization of academia in some countries and subject areas with consequent negative effects. Academic jobs have become considered low-status, and salaries have fallen way behind other fields. The increase in mass higher education, the proliferation of universities and institutions of higher learning, and the pro-letarianization of academia has resulted in the role of academic staff becoming increasingly that of adviser rather than tutor, with even remedial teaching being given. We may even ask whether there is a tendency towards a culture of mothering, a process exacerbated by the compartmentalization of courses and the fragmentation of knowledge that follows in its wake. Mothering has traditionally not been the role of a university, and should not be so. In this sphere, women's entrance into the arena should not change intellectual and academic criteria.

Academia needs leaders who are prepared to modernize, but not at the expense of quality or depth of knowledge. The ideal leader will be in contact with the world outside academia, but not be controlled by it. She or he will utilize market forces where applicable, but not be a slave to them. These are some of the requirements that must be in place before we can encourage women to aim at senior positions, or younger women and men to enter the academic professions. The next century is unlikely to see people who are willing to make the personal sacrifices demanded of an academic position at present. The élitist universities will always survive as seats of learning and research, but we must ask whether the non-élitist, or those who do not choose to specialize in a few fields, will survive in the next century.

Bibliography

Coates, J. (ed.) 1998. *Language and Gender: A Reader*. Oxford, Blackwell.

Gerhardi, S. 1995. *Gender, Symbolism and Organizational Change*. London, Sage.

Hzin, C.; Newman, J. (eds) 1995. *Gender, Culture and Organizational Change. Putting Theory into Practice*. London, Routledge.

Irigaray, L. 1993. *je, tu, nous. Toward a Culture of Difference*. (Translated by Alison Martin). London and New York, Routledge.

Ledwith, S.; Colgan, F. (eds) 1996. *Women in Organisations. Challenging Gender Politics.* London, Macmillan.

Lips, H.M. 1998. *Attraction and Ambivalence: Gendered Perceptions of Power.* <http://www.runet.edu/-gstudies/keyintro.html>

Time, 24 May 1999. 'The Global Leadership Challenge'.

INDEX